A VILLAG? in Croxl

"When the Mill Field Grew Turnips"
By
Frank Paddick

Front cover: celebrating the coronation of George V on the Green, 1911
Back cover: 'Neggy' Wilson's memorial bench beneath the George V jubilee oak and Providence Hall, the Green.

Published in Great Britain by

Rickmansworth Historical Society
http://rickmansworthhistoricalsociety.btck.co.uk/

First published – 2012

ISBN number 978-0-9544583-2-4

**Printed in the United Kingdom
by Hobbs the Printers Ltd,
Totton, Hampshire**

A VILLAGE BOYHOOD
In Croxley Green
"When the Mill Field Grew Turnips"

By
Frank Paddick

Edited by Brian Thomson
Illustrated by Alison Lee

Contents   Page

❧ *PREFACE* ❧

Frank Paddick was born on 12 December 1909, the ninth of eleven children. The family lived at 262 New Road, Croxley Green. They had moved from Rickmansworth some time after 1901 and Frank's father Walter worked as a mill hand at Dickinson's Croxley Mill. Finding two bedrooms a bit cramped for such a large family, they moved across to a larger house at number 283 in about 1913. Frank mentions the move in the second chapter of this book.

The Paddick family 16 May 1916. Frank is second from right in the front row.

Frank left the school in Watford Road at the age of 13 and became an apprentice electrician at a firm in Northwood. Subsequently, he worked for Pitkins when they were building the houses in Frankland Road. Building stopped at the outbreak of war in 1939 and Frank joined Croxley Mill, where a number of the family were employed. His elder brother, Frederick, became the chief paper maker at Croxley and went on to manage Nash Mills for John Dickinson and Co.. Frank suffered from ill health for many years. Bronchitis and smoking led to emphysema which made physical activity increasingly difficult. Fortunately, the Mill continued to employ him on light duties in spite of his illness. Frank and his family continued to live at 283 New Road until his death in 1965 at the age of 55.

It is our good fortune that Frank's ill health did not stop him from pursuing his interest in local history. He wrote several articles about Croxley for the *Dickinson Review* including a piece about the Croxley Mummers. Frank was one of the founders and an enthusiastic Mummer for many years. He undertook painstaking research into a range of topics that interested him and published thoughtful articles in the *Rickmansworth Historian* from 1962 until his death. The topics included the use of token coinage in Rickmansworth,[1] Providence Hall,[2] Redheath,[3] Parrotts,[4] Smoky Hall[5] and the Mummers.[6] Frank was also closely involved in recording memories of 'Neggy' Wilson, Headmaster of Croxley Boys' School.[7] 'Neggy' had a great influence on many of his pupils, including Frank.

Allan Leach, editor of the *Rickmansworth Historian*, wrote an affectionate tribute,[8] in which he explains that it was when Frank became too ill to carry out his research that he turned to recording his memories of Croxley during his boyhood. According to Allan: -
> When it was finished Frank, like any other author, wondered what to do with it. It was too long for his employer's magazine, and while there are periodicals which would gladly have printed it, he was too uncertain of his abilities to send it to them. In 1956 the B.B.C. had broadcast a short programme on the Croxley Mummers and Frank, of course, had taken part in it. He remembered its producer, Jack Singleton, as being the kind of

[1] 'The money-makers of Rickmansworth,' *Rickmansworth Historian* 3, 1962, pp.33-36
[2] 'The mark of Joseph Doll,' *RH* 4, 1962, pp.51-58
[3] *RH* 5, 1963, pp.91-95 and 9, 1965, pp. 215-217
[4] *RH* 6, 1963, pp.107-112
[5] *RH* 7, 1964, pp.134-140
[6] *RH* 8, 1964, pp.175-184
[7] 'As though it were yesterday.' *RH* 5, 1963, pp.75-82, and 'But never to his face.' *RH* 8, 1964, pp.164-167
[8] *RH* 11, 1966, pp. 261-267

man to take an interest in local topics, and sent the manuscript to him. That done, Frank, recovering now, expected to hear no more. What happened was that he was invited to visit Great Portland Street and record his script[9] as a talk, and on 13 February 1961 the greater part of it was broadcast in the London Home Service.

In late 1963 Frank's illness was such that he was confined to bed. With Allan's encouragement and practical help, he added to the story of his childhood and created this book. In Allan's words: -

He remained a countryman amid the spread of suburbia, and while he regretted the change, he took a historian's pleasure in conjuring up the Croxley he had known as a boy, or the village as it had been in earlier times.

Frank writes of a time, around 1920, when Croxley Green was a village of about 2,000 people. Dickinson's mill had pulled Croxley's centre of gravity away from the Green along New Road, which in those days had many more shops than it does today. See the map on page 8 which locates the places described in these pages. The paper mill provided employment but the countryside was still close by. Frank describes Croxley then as an 'industrial island in a sea of great estates, surrounded as we were by the domain of my Lords of Essex, Clarendon and Ebury'. By the time he was writing in the 1960s, things had changed greatly with the advent of Metroland's suburban housing and the selling off of the great estates. The changes are still greater today, 30 years after the closure of Dickinson's mill, and when the last of Croxley's farms at Killingdown seems destined to become another housing estate. Consequently, Frank's writings provide us with a window on a time that is long gone but which still leaves its traces if you look for them.

Frank includes stories about people who would have been well known in Croxley at the time. In a few cases he changed their names to avoid embarrassment.

I am grateful to Richard and Keith Paddick for making available Frank's original typescript and for their help and support in producing this volume. Thanks are also due to Alison Lee for her splendid drawings, to Heather Falvey, for her help with editing and to Jane Brading for help

---

[9] 'When the mill field grew turnips' published in the first number of the *Rickmansworth Historian*, 1961, pp.6-8

with typing. I am grateful to those who have provided the illustrations which are listed on page 105.

Brian Thomson   March 2011

Whippendell woods

7

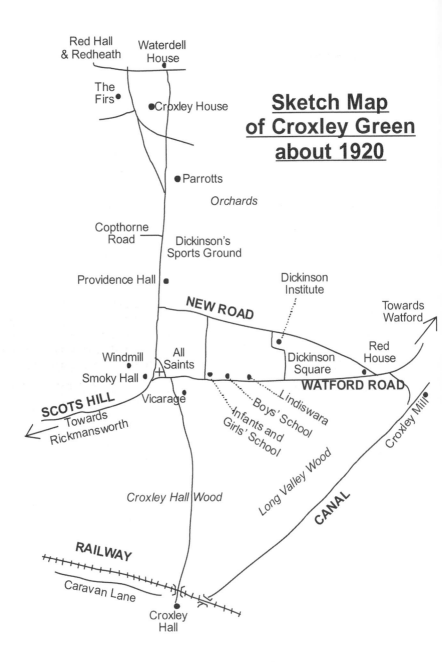

Red Hall & Redheath

Waterdell House

The Firs

Croxley House

Sketch Map of Croxley Green about 1920

Parrotts

Orchards

Copthorne Road

Dickinson's Sports Ground

Dickinson Institute

Towards Watford

Providence Hall

NEW ROAD

Red House

Windmill

All Saints

Dickinson Square

WATFORD ROAD

Smoky Hall

Lindiswara

SCOTS HILL

Vicarage

Boys' School

Towards Rickmansworth

Infants and Girls' School

Long Valley Wood

CANAL

Croxley Mill

Croxley Hall Wood

RAILWAY

Caravan Lane

Croxley Hall

8

CHAPTER ONE

Come, come, come along

The cowman's call seemed merely to add to the noise and confusion as his herd gathered momentum through our long village street. Perhaps it was the sound of their hooves on the metalled surface, perhaps knowing that they were nearing the milking sheds and relief for their overburdened udders, but they increased their pace with every step they took. The cows appeared to reserve their natural functions until they felt the hard surface beneath their hooves, for now the 'cowflabs' fell thick and fast on road and pavement, splashing walls, fences and gates in passing.

Old ladies, meeting the cows head on, found new wings for aching legs and rapidly disappeared down paths and alleyways, or opened a front garden gate and waited till the herd went by. A few minutes and they had 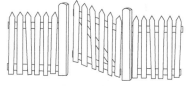 passed, leaving a trail which repelled the fastidious and delighted the small boys – accustomed to adding to their meagre pocket money by dunging in the streets.

Foster's
Dairy
New Road

Twice daily the cows steadily chewed their way to the gateway of the moor, patiently awaiting the arrival of the cowman. Slowly, almost reluctantly, they left the moor, and were heedless of his 'Come, come, come, come along', wisely refusing to be hurried while they climbed the steep hill from the moor to where our village street ('Cow Lane' it used to be called) led to the farm. The gentler gradient of the street itself, however, really helped them to get into their stride.

Into the village, too, came great barge horses, with an occasional mule or donkey, seeking stabling at public house or other premises which catered for their needs. Barges and longboats in those days carried most of the paper mill's raw materials of esparto grass and woodpulp from the ships in the Thames and coal from the midland collieries.

John Dickinson's Croxley Mill

The smell of bleach and boiling esparto grass borne on the east wind wafted up the valley from the mill and mingled with the other village smells which seemed so natural a part of life at that time of day. Our great mill chimney belched forth its black smoke into the sky, and

10

seemed to probe the very heavens. Two hundred feet! Was anything taller than this? We doubted it. We were told that the Eiffel Tower was over nine hundred feet high, but we would like to see it first. St. Paul's was four hundred feet high, two hundred feet higher than our chimney, maybe, but it didn't look it. Elsewhere little children might cry for the moon, but with us they said of a dissatisfied child, 'He will want the top brick off the mill chimney next' and we all knew that was almost as unattainable. From time to time the steeplejacks would arrive to repair the chimney and we gazed on them with childish awe, marvelling at their courage. We were surprised to see how ordinary they looked.

Queen Victoria had closed her eyes for the last time some eight years before I first opened mine. Before I could sit up and take notice, her son Edward the seventh had departed to join his mother in their last resting place at Windsor. So long had been her reign and so great her influence on the lives of her subjects that she still seemed to dominate them. Her portrait still adorned the walls of many of our cottage homes and smiled, smirked or sneered at the occupants, according to the eye of the beholder.

Her picture may only have hung in some of the cottages, but her repressive shade fell across the hearths of all. Valances still draped the beds and washstand to hide the legs from the vulgar gaze and many a workman wore a threadbare shirt while his wife pandered to these absurdities.

King Edward's reign seemed but a brief interlude. One would hear the occasional mention of 'Teddy', but I do not recall anyone referring to Victoria as 'Vicky': that would have been considered much too familiar.

Life seemed settled, timeless and unalterable, each day like the day that went before it. Calendars and clocks seemed a superfluity in these far-off times. We knew the quiet rhythm of tomorrow would be but another yesterday or today.

A trinity of bells governed the lives of all but the very old and the very young. Their unmelodious message few dared or wished to ignore. The church bell called the faithful to prayer, the school bell the unwilling to school, and the bell of our paper mill urged, let us hope, the eager to work.

While I was still a very tiny child the chug-chugging which heralded the approach of an aeroplane brought everyone out of their houses. These were the early days of aviation, and aeroplanes were rarely seen. I managed to get to the garden fields at the back of my home, where an excited crowd had assembled. The pilot was clearly visible to us but I have no idea at what height he was flying. One of the men mentioned a thousand feet, and the old chap near whose plot of ground we had gathered leaned on his fork long enough to say, with a look of astonishment, 'What, five times higher 'n the mill chimney?', and then resumed his digging, chuckling with amused disbelief.

'Five times higher than the mill chimney'. It was the yardstick by which we measured heights.

Croxley Mill 1929

❦❦❦ CHAPTER TWO ❦❦❦

Early years - family life in New Road

New Road, Croxley Green

When night began to fall, great flocks of peewits, which then nested on the moor and the marshy lands down in the valley, flew round and round the village. These bonny birds lazily looped, tumbled and called to each other while they took their twilight flight before settling down for the night. Occasionally they would continue to circle overhead long after darkness had enveloped the village, while their cries became more frequent and seemed to contain a note of fear. The old people, hearing the birds' cries, would shake their heads and say, 'somebody or something is on the moor tonight – the peewits are afraid to go down to roost.' But a peewit cannot fly at night, and finally overcoming their fears they went down to roost and their cries gradually died away.

The tiny terraced cottage where I was born seemed comfortable, warm and secure. With two rooms up and two downstairs it was impossible to be lonely, and even outdoors the nearness of the neighbours added to the togetherness and made us all one with each other. The rich red brocade curtains, a present from my grandfather,

were perhaps out of place in our tiny living room. With the red plush table cloth, red crocheted mantleborder and red drapes on either side of the tiny living room range, they seemed, when the day's work was over, to reflect the firelight's glow.

The framed memorial card for my grandmother, who had died some years before my birth, hung upon the wall. She had been buried in the churchyard of a neighbouring village. Sometimes an elder brother or sister with nothing more entertaining to do would begin to read it aloud. They seldom got beyond this line of the verse –

'The cup was bitter, the pain severe.....'[10]

before my mother would call out, 'Oh, don't read that again', but despite this I must have heard it many times, and fell to pondering the mystery of death at a very early age.

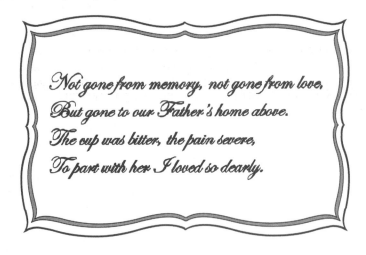

Not gone from memory, not gone from love,
But gone to our Father's home above.
The cup was bitter, the pain severe,
To part with her I loved so dearly.

---

[10] This is a four-line verse that was frequently carved on headstones and, as here, written on memorial cards.

I can remember only one cause for fear in that tiny cottage home. We had only oil for lighting, and my mother lived in constant dread of the oil lamp being knocked over. As soon as the light began to fade on the short winter's day the lamp was placed in the middle of the living room table, and from then till bedtime our movements seemed restricted by the fear of it. My mother's fears were not unfounded, for many families had perished, many homes been destroyed, by children's frolics spilling the oil from these lamps.

About the time of my third birthday we moved. The new house, not far from the old one, seemed a vast place to me. Still only a small cottage, it boasted another bedroom, and all the rooms were much larger than in our old home. The oil lamp was no longer needed here, for we now had gas lights. That in the living room consisted of a brass tube about a yard long, and hissed and spluttered whilst it burned. It was happily out of reach of childish hands. The fear of the oil lamp was no more, but it was replaced for me by a far greater one, and one that was present not for just an hour or so on a winter's evening, but at all hours of the day and night, in every room in the house.

Unknown to the rest of my family, my mother and father, brothers and sisters, the house was inhabited by a man and a dog. They never revealed themselves to anyone but me, and by some subtle, sinister means they conveyed to me that I was not to tell anyone else of their presence. So great was the terror they had managed to instill in me that I never did. The man, a short plumpish person with a face which, under any other

circumstances might have been jolly, could have been a gamekeeper, groom, or coachman. He was always dressed in the same way, with breeches, sports coat and highly polished black leather gaiters.

The dog, a black Labrador, was always at his side and seated on its haunches, making it almost as tall as the man: never once did I see the creature on all fours. This precious pair had no ghost-like habits of gradually fading or appearing, they were either there or not, and much too often for my peace of mind they were there. If my mother left the room they were before me, indicating in some strange manner that I was to go, and indeed I needed no prodding to depart, but fled in terror the moment I was left alone. They never spoke, and I do mean they, for I was convinced the dog could have done so if it wished. I sensed in some way that the dog was the stronger of the two, and the cause of these visitations.

There was a passage from the front door and an upstairs landing, both divided by match-boarding from the rooms. This wooden partition and the staircase were all stained dark, while the walls had been papered with dark green squares, making this part of the house especially gloomy. Upstairs landing and downstairs passage were some three or four yards long, but had they been so many miles they could not have seemed longer to me. If ever a knock came at the front door, or I was sent into the front room, they were there barring my path: the plump man and the dog with its baleful eyes and dribbling jaws, and I recoiled in horror, my mission unaccomplished.

I must have been a great nuisance to my mother, with my reluctance to leave her side, my determination never to be alone for one moment. It is now some fifty years since I saw this pair, but so deeply are they graven on my mind that I have only to think of them to see them clearly before me.

I longed then for the evening, when the rest of the family were at home and man and dog stayed hidden away. Evening round the fire has always been a time of great joy to me, when, the day's work over, people seemed to relax after the evening meal.

The large kitchen range played a great part of the life of the housewife at that time and was the cause of much drudgery. The flues required frequent cleaning-out with flue brush and scraper; the whole range was carefully black-leaded every day, and the steel parts shone like glass after the daily rubbing with the emery cloth. Fenders, fire irons and fire-guards all had the emery paper applied to them with equal vigour, and the hearth was constantly being rewhitened with hearthstone. Our kitchen range was supposed to provide hot water too. It had the fire in the middle, oven on one side, and boiler on the other. The boiler had no pipes attached, and was filled by the simple method of pouring water in from jug or kettle. On the front of the range at the bottom of the boiler was a small brass tap, from which one drew the hot water. The washer of this tap was worn, and in need of renewal. About four o'clock in the afternoon my mother would fill up the boiler ready for the family to take their evening wash, and the steady drip of water soon destroyed the virgin whiteness of the hearth. A cup or tin placed in the hearth to catch the drips would have been a simple solution and my mother, a resourceful woman, must have been well aware of this. I think it was left to drip to shame my father, for he was always 'going to see to it tomorrow', or 'had spoken to somebody about a new washer'. Then in my fourth year, it was with a feeling of irritation and discomfort that I watched the dry whiteness of the hearth turn into the greyness of a wet one.

The evening meal over, the water was soon drawn off by various members of the family, and with the heat from the fire the hearth soon returned to its original whiteness. Soon the boiler lining sprang a leak which made it impossible to use at all, and the brass tap became just a bright ornament on the shining black face of the kitchen range.

Around about this time the family bought a gramophone. My previous musical experience had consisted of listening to a neighbour's phonograph, but now we had a much superior machine of our own. It was in constant use, for even when my own brothers and sisters temporarily tired of turning the handle there were always some friends or neighbours popping in to sit enthralled and mystified while the black record whirred around.

Today we take television, radio and the record player for granted, and few pause to wonder. Much of the pleasure in the early gramophone days was in wondering how voices came out of the horn at all.

Ta-Ra-Ra-Boom-De-Ay[11] was beginning to lose some of its popularity about this time, and the earliest record I can remember was about a little boy who had found a penny, with which he bought a packet of cigarettes. The verse I have forgotten, but the chorus went something like this:-

> *Five cigarettes in a dainty little packet,*
> *Five cigarettes which cost one D;[12]*
> *Five little pains underneath his jacket;*
> *Five wobbles in his little Mary.*
> *Five little whiffs – five little jiffs.*
> *He was lying on the tramway line,*
> *Wishing he could reach the cable,*
> *He was greener than the label,*
> *And a copper stole his last Woodbine.*

This ditty was sung with great gusto by old and young alike. Another song which I remember from these days was: -

> *I do love you my Orange girl, indeed I do,*
> *For I never met a girl that's better, ever since I met you.*
> *If you'll only leave your orange grove and say 'I will',*
> *Then the bells will soon be ringing, swinging,*
> > *in the church of old Seville.*

Still the quiet way of life flowed on. Each morning shortly after breakfast the butcher came and discussed the day's meat, which would soon be delivered by the butcher's boy. The milkman made three daily deliveries: early morning, mid-day and about four in the afternoon. His horse knew each customer, and stopped outside their gates, and every customer knew the horse. The milk was carried in great churns, transferred into hand cans on the milk float and then measured out with a half-pint scoop into the jugs which had been left on window-sill or doorstep.

Both man and horse were of regular habits, and old Mrs. Howard who lived next door to us took full advantage of this, the horse's daily tribute being speedily placed on her garden.

---

[11] A popular music hall song.

[12] D, or more usually d, was the abbreviation for a penny.

Times, however, change, and after years of regular delivery by both man and beast the milkman obtained a new customer a few houses along the road, and found it more convenient to stop his cart there.

The first morning of the new stopping-place my neighbour emerged as usual, only to find that the new customer, another old lady, had beaten her to the post and secured the coveted prize.

After returning every morning for a fortnight with an empty pail she had reached breaking-point, and apostrophised the milkman thus: 'Mr Kinch,[13] I have been your customer for ten years, and during the whole of that time your horse has stopped outside my house and obliged me. If you think it fair that a new customer to the locality should have what I have always regarded as my little bonus, and don't arrange for your horse to stop outside my gate as it did before she came, I'm afraid I must go elsewhere for my milk.'

A decade had passed since the Boer war, but Ladysmith and Mafeking[14] were constantly being recalled. Redvers Buller, Lord Roberts and Kitchener[15] were still the great heroes and Oom Paul Kruger[16] a bogey-man with whom many a wayward child was threatened. But these heroes were soon to be replaced with others. Events were beginning to shape which dwarfed the Boer War, and only Kitchener's name would remain on people's lips.

I first became aware while listening to a conversation between my mother and a Mrs Tullet, a distant relation of my father's, that something was happening which distressed my elders. A new name had crept into their talk, one which I hadn't heard before: 'The Kaiser'. My mother seemed to have a presentiment of the blood-bath of the next few years,[17] but Mrs Tullet dismissed her fears with scorn.

---

[13] The Kinch family owned the dairy in New Road, subsequently Foster's, and now occupied by James Peddle Undertakers. See page 8 photo.

[14] British victories in 1900.

[15] British generals and national heroes during the Boer War.

[16] Leader of Boer resistance against the British.

[17] Three of Frank's older brothers, Henry, James and Frederick, served in the forces during the First World War. Their names are listed with others from Croxley Green on All Saints' 'Shrine'.

'Don't you bother about him,' said Mrs Tullet, 'he's only an upstart. It's a pity Queen Victoria wasn't still with us, she'd soon put him in his place. She'd give him Kaiser!'

'But look what they've done to the Belgians,' replied my mother.

'Belgium ain't British – you can't take any notice of them. Once Kitchener gets over there,' continued Mrs Tullet, 'they'll all bolt. K of K[18] won't stand any of their nonsense.'

I had found the situation confusing enough, with all the new names being bandied around – Belgians, French, Germans, The Kaiser – and I devoutly hoped it wouldn't be long before Kitchener arrived and 'they all bolted'.

Mrs Tullet and her husband were better off than us, and as it is, of course, well known that one's wisdom and knowledge of current affairs is in proportion to one's property, my mother refrained from further comment.

The gramophone was being overworked now, patriotic songs being much in demand. There were, of course, some lighter songs, and one which I remember went like this: -

Since poor Father joined the Territorials
Ours is a happy, happy, home.
He wakes us up in the middle of the night
And says we must all be prepared to fight.
He puts poor mother in the dustbin
To stand on sentry guard.
And there's me and brother John
With our little night-shirts on.
Marching round the old backyard.

Fortunately my father didn't join the Territorials, and I was spared the indignity of marching up the old backyard in my nightshirt, but young as I was I did do a little marching[19]. Just along the road there lived an old gentleman who, still with the cheers of Mafeking ringing in

---

[18] Lord Kitchener of Khartoum.

[19] The author was only four and a half at the outbreak of war. The patriotism he describes was typical of feelings during the early stages of the conflict.

his ears, regarded the war with enthusiasm. He had purchased a dozen or two little Union Jacks, and paraded the children of the neighbourhood round and round, while we endlessly sang 'The soldiers of the Queen'. He was to pay a heavy price for his patriotism. His two sons, among the early volunteers to cross the Channel, were also among the first of our village boys to make the 'supreme sacrifice'.[20]

Then, while many of our village men heard and responded to the bugle's call, I found the school bell had begun to ring for me. Came the Monday morning when my elder sister clasped my little hand in hers and proudly presented me to the Infants' School Headmistress.

---

[20] The First World War was momentous and tragic for the people of Croxley Green. Almost every family was affected in one way or another. 57 Croxley men died, as recorded on the war memorial, and 355 served with the military, as listed on All Saints' 'Shrine'. Many of those who survived were deeply marked by their experience. There were five Croxley families who suffered the loss of two sons killed in the fighting. Three of them (Goodman, Mead and Woollams) lived in New Road (1911 census).

🍂🍃 CHAPTER THREE 🍃🍂

Schooldays begin[21]

And now I was thrust into the harsh world of the school play-ground: a world in which few holds are barred, at least by the school-children. A world in which all sham and pretension disappear, and one's physical and mental imperfections are not only revealed but mercilessly exploited by fellow-pupils. The plump child becomes 'fatty', 'tubby', 'podgy' and the thin one 'skinny'. An eye defect may earn you the title of 'boss eye', and should you have a tendency towards a long nose you straightway become 'snouthy' or 'nosy'. You may as easily become 'old bandy legs', 'knock knees', or 'pigeon toes' from the moment you first set foot in the playground, and this can remain with you for the rest of your school-days – and often far beyond them. The tougher child will not mind this, but the sensitive one may be made very unhappy.

Yorke Road School

---

[21] Chapters 3 and 4 were published in the *Rickmansworth Historian* 17, 1969, p.428-433

Our infant school and girls' school[22] were side by side, and we shared the same playground and toilets. The girls stayed at school until their fourteenth birthday and the tiny children were at a great disadvantage. At playtime we always seemed in the way of the big girls. Every game they played required large portions of the playground: skipping-ropes whirred round to the cry of 'Salt, mustard, vinegar, pepper...', and one risked entanglement in them and a push or smack from the girls if one ventured too near.

Another great favourite was Hopscotch, and wherever a grid was chalked out on the tarmac was private property, which one crossed at one's peril.

We like to think of the schoolgirl as being kindly, sweet and tolerant, and individually many of them are. Collectively, however, they can be just as cruel and intolerant as their brothers. One of my earliest memories of school is of a crowd of girls surrounding one little girl, who sobbed as they chanted:

> Tell tale tit,
> Give your tongue a slit
> And all the little puppy-dogs
> Shall have a little bit.

This rhyme was a great favourite with boys and girls, and was constantly to be heard when some child was considered guilty of tale-bearing.

There seemed to be no place in the play-ground for the tiny child, and we spent much of our time leaning against the school wall or the fence. If one of us found a snail, worm, beetle or some other crawling creature, it became an object of great interest to us, and we huddled round to watch its movements, or timidly prod it with a twig.

The iron railing which separated our play-ground from the pavement of the road seemed to have been designed to trap small children. They were separated by the exact width of the average child's hand, and it was a regular happening for a child seeking to retrieve a ball or some other object from the road to get his head wedged between the bars. This had occurred with such frequency for years that the teachers

---

[22] At the corner of Yorke Road and Watford Road

23

had become quite skilled in extricating their charges. Sometimes a child more fat-headed than his fellows would be more difficult to set free, and a passer-by recognising the child would hasten to fetch its mother, who would soon arrive and add to the general confusion. Fat-headed or otherwise, however, all the victims were eventually released without apparent harm.

Many of the children carried Poppy-shows. These were small pieces of glass, some two or three inches square, behind which had been pressed a variety of small flowers. A paper flap covered the glass, and would be lifted to reveal the flowers when another child had paid one pin, the charge for viewing. This was requested by the verse:

A pin to see the poppy-show,
A pin to see them die,
A pin to see an old man
Just riding in the sky.

Against the school wall leaned dozens of hoops of all sizes, which the children were not allowed to bowl in the play-ground. In those traffic-free days, when most vehicles were horse-drawn and there was only an occasional motor-car, we gaily bowled our hoops to school. Most of the boys had hoops of metal, made by the local blacksmith. If these broke or got twisted out of  shape they could be taken back to the smithy and reconditioned for twopence. These metal hoops were of a uniform size, about a yard in diameter. The girls had wooden hoops, and these varied from tiny ones about a foot in diameter to extra-large ones some four or five feet high.

Each child had a skimmer. This was a wooden handle with a metal hook on the end. We used the wooden handle to hit the hoop when propelling it along the road, and the metal hook to put round the hoop and hold it back when it threatened to go too fast for its pursuing owner.

Many games were played with these hoops. Sometimes the girls with the largest hoops ran through them, gave the hoop another knock onwards and ran through it again. They would have competitions to see who could run through the greatest number of times without either stopping or knocking the hoop over. At other times small hoops would be bowled through large hoops, and sometimes there would be crashes between hoops, with quarrels breaking out between the owners. Crashes were usually caused quite deliberately by the boys! Great fun was had by all of us, and it was a great sight to see droves of children bowling hoops of all sizes on their way to school.

Children outside the Co-op on New Road

One game in which we all joined, large and small alike, was 'Oranges and Lemons'. Two of the big girls would be chosen to be 'Orange' and 'Lemon', and would stand making an archway of their arms. The remainder of us, formed into a column, would pass under the arch as we all sang the old rhyme:

Oranges and Lemons,
Say the bells of St. Clement's
You owe me five farth'ngs,
Say the bells of St. Martin's
When will you pay me,
Say the bells of Old Bailey,
When I grow rich,
Say the bells of Shoreditch.

25

When will that be?
Say the bells of Stepney.
I'm sure I don't know,
Says the great bell of Bow.
Here comes a candle to light you to bed.
Here comes a chopper to chop off your head.
Chop, chop, chop!

And down would come the arms of the two big girls on whichever of us was underneath. The trapped (or 'chopped') child was then given the choice of being either 'Orange' or 'Lemon' and, having chosen, went to stand behind the appropriate side of the archway. Then it all began again until the next player was 'chopped', and so on until we were all drawn up in lines behind the original pair. Then came a tug-of-war to decide the winners, each of us clasping both arms round the waist of the child in front and pulling until victors and vanquished alike collapsed in a panting heap.

But I had not come to school to stay in the play-ground. My business was the classroom, and to the babies' class I was taken by the school governess. Children at that time did not have to wait for a new term to begin school: they began their education when their mothers were ready to send them. Consequently they made their entrances alone, and not in the company of other pupils. The day's work had already begun when the governess ushered me into the classroom, and while my fellow-scholars continued with their singing of 'All things bright and beautiful', and the two teachers discussed me, I was able to stare about at what was to me an entirely new world.

The walls were lined with crayon drawings. Window-sills, tables, shelves, cupboard-tops, and every available space were crowded with jam-jars full of flowers, jars of tadpoles, shells, and grotesque plasticine animals – my future classmates' first attempts at modelling. The class teacher, Miss Jones, was a kindly spinster who had become prematurely old while attending to other people's children. She had now been in the school long enough to have taught the parents of many of her present children in the very same classroom.

The hymn-singing, deprived of the support of Miss Jones, had now petered out, and the school governess took her leave. Turning to me, Miss Jones, asked if there was any child in the class that I knew. I indicated a boy in the front row who lived a few doors from my home,

26

and room was soon made for me at his side on the long bench, which accommodated some half-a-dozen children.

Mary Brown's class Yorke Road, 1915.

My first lesson was to be writing, and each of us was given a tray filled with sand. The teacher then drew, slowly and carefully, a letter in white chalk on the blackboard, and we all copied the shape in our sand-trays with our fingers. Much of our time seemed to be occupied with the sand-trays, or in making men or animals in plasticine.

Miss Jones seemed to spend a lot of time in attending to ailing children. Coughs and sneezes, and all baby complaints seemed prevalent. At the back of the classroom, beside the cupboard, was folded a large red felt curtain. This had at some time been used for dividing a classroom, but was now frequently used as a temporary bed for some complaining child. Came the morning when I, too, found myself being made comfortable there, but I was conscious that too many bilious babes had rested there before me and, young as I was, I vowed to avoid this corner in future.

27

Perhaps the best teachers are those whom we remember least. When a child is absorbed with the personality of his teacher, can he be concentrating on his lessons? In any event, I moved next into the class taken by the school governess, and I have only the vaguest recollections of the time I spent there. The trays of sand had been left behind, and we now graduated to the dignity of slate and slate-pencil.

The chief business of the infants seemed to be to chant the alphabet and the numbers from one to a hundred. This chanting was continually interrupted by the governess, to ask one child or another which letter came after another. By this method most of the children could repeat the alphabet and count long before either of these accomplishments had any real meaning to them. On certain afternoons the girls would have sewing lessons, and while they were employed with needle and thread the boys were given paper and paste, with which to make little models. During these lessons the governess spent much of her time mixing with the class, and giving a hand to both girls and boys when either were in difficulties with their tasks.

CHAPTER FOUR

Third year at the Infants' School

There were three classes in our Infants' School, and from the third and last of these one moved either next door to the Girls' School, or a little lower down the road to the Boys' School.

This third class was taught by Nan Downe, and she ruled it with a rod of iron, or to be more exact, of wood. The weapon she used, and used with considerable dexterity, was the pointer. Designed for pointing to the lesson on the blackboard, in her hands this became an effective weapon with which she rapped the hands and heads of her pupils on the slightest provocation. The class was in a constant state of turmoil: warned 'not to fiddle with something under the desk' and 'not to fidget', and either of these offences bringing the pointer down on the offender. There were no favourites: it was used on boys and girls alike; Nan rapped the blackboard, her desk, and ours to draw our attention.

I cannot remember seeing her without the pointer. She entered the classroom carrying it, and presumably left again with it. I have vivid memories of her coming into class, but cannot recall her leaving; her entrance was always perfectly timed. The school governess taught the class in the next room to Nan's, and the latter would remain in conversation with her until the class, responding to the handbell's ring, had assembled. She did not have to tell the class to be quiet: the babble of childish talk ceased the moment she opened the door with the dreaded pointer poised at the ready.

In Nan Downe's class I not only acquired the rudiments of the three Rs, but also became conscious of the opposite sex. It was dawning on me that little girls were different from little boys. Not only were little girls beginning to interest me, but a big girl too, for despite her constant application of the pointer, I was fascinated by Nan Downe. Perhaps it was not so much Nan that interested me as her mode of dress. She wore a long blue frock which reached to her ankles, but most attractive to at least one small boy was her sash. This was a bright red, some four or five inches wide. It was wound round her waist, and the two ends followed her dress down to her ankles. Her rapid motions and habit of darting about the classroom kept the sash-ends continually flying. I think it must have been the sash which attracted me to Nan, for I

29

remember asking my mother why she didn't wear one like it. When, during the mid-morning gossip, my mother repeated this to some of the neighbours they all had a good, long, laugh. As one of them said, 'We should look well, blacking the grates and whitening the hearth in one of them things'. (Normal wear for this job was a coarse apron, which hung behind the backhouse door when there was no heavy work to be done.)

The children took the only way they knew of getting back at Nan Downe for her strictness and her accuracy with the pointer: they made up rhymes about her and chanted them when she was out of hearing: -

> *We'll ask Nan Downe to tea,*
> *And all her family.*
> *If she don't come we'll tickle her bum*
> *With a stick of celery.*

> *Old Nan Downe she went to town*
> *To buy a pair of breeches,*
> *She got behind a cart, and let such a fart*
> *She busted all her stitches.*

> *Old Nan Downe she went to town,*
> *And where d'you think they found her?*
> *Behind the pump, a'scratching her rump*
> *And all the people round her.*

I was no better than the others, but because these verses were directed at Nan, for whom I had formed some attachment, I found them inexpressibly vulgar.

There were two little girls in the class who constantly distracted me from Nan Downe's teaching: Barbara and Gwendoline. Barbara, with her fair ringlets and wide blue eyes, had a doll-like prettiness which, like a doll's could soon be destroyed. Living with two maiden aunts, Barbara arrived at school, each morning looking as if she had just been taken out of her box. Perhaps it was due to some cattiness on the part of the other girls, but as the day wore on she seemed to become somewhat bedraggled. Given to easy tears she seemed frequently in trouble.

But over and above these I loved Gwendoline best of all. With her chestnut hair, brown eyes and sturdy figure, Gwen was the complete opposite of Barbara in every way. Of a placid and equable disposition, it was impossible to ruffle her.

From time to time we read in the national press of some schoolgirl being sent home because the heels of her shoes were considered by her headmistress to be too high, her dress unbecoming, or her hair style unsuitable for one of her age. In the early years of the century the chief bone of contention between mistress and pupil was the pinafore.

Infants class at Yorke Road School

Authority had decreed that all girls attending school must wear a clean pinafore. Most of the mothers respected this ruling, and their daughters arrived daily all prim and proper, with stiffly starched pinnies. Occasionally some mother in a rebellious mood, or perhaps overburdened with a large family and all the domestic chores inseparable from the age, would send her daughter to school without her pinafore – when she would promptly be sent back home. This sometimes led to wordy warfare between parents and teachers.

The pinafore was the mark of respectability: the forerunner for girls of the school uniform. We boys had for long been clad in Eton collar, Norfolk jacket and knickerbockers, but about this time a new fashion arrived for us: short knickers, with bare knees and turned-down stockings. The knees of knickerbockers were very vulnerable to wear and tear when scraped down walls and trees or crawled upon in the course of some game. They were frequently in need of repair. Despite this, some of our parents were unwilling to see us make the change, for bare knees, it was felt, were against nature, and we should all become victims of colds, chills, and countless other evils.

The change duly came, and we shed the now old-fashioned clothes. The Eton collar and Norfolk jacket were willingly surrendered, for their restrictive grip had long been the bane of small boys. But knickerbockers were different. Their baggy knees had for long been the traditional storing place for chestnuts, walnuts, apples and pears: mainly scrumped from the local orchards. To stow a cargo required considerable skill, for to overload was to court disaster and entail the wearer walking bandy-legged, and if pursued by an angry farmer he had quickly to bend down, loose the knee buttons, and jettison the load as he ran. A great treat for the bystander to watch, with the fruit streaming from the now open knees as the boy gained speed.

We were experts on the local apples, and could place any orchard with two bites and state the exact tree with three, so we had very mixed feelings about parting with our knickerbockers. Not, perhaps, for reasons as reputable as our parents', but for both parents and sons 'to bare or not to bare' the knees became a burning question.

Church service in a Croxley orchard

CHAPTER FIVE

Croxley Boys' School

At the beginning of a new term the scholars who were 'going up' were called from their desks by Nan Downe and marched into the playground for a final inspection by the Headmistress. This was goodbye to co-education;[23] goodbye to pretty, distracting, girls' faces; goodbye for many boys to the mischievous joy of pulling pigtails and loosening the bows of ribbon from girls' hair. Goodbye, too, to Nan Downe's flying sash and her ever-ready pointer.

For the girls the change meant just a transfer to another part of the same building, for they would continue to use the same playground. For the boys there was a march of a hundred yards or so down the road. I was already familiar with the outside of the boys' school[24] and had long dreamed of the time when I should become a pupil there. The building clad in its mantle of ivy and creeper could easily have been converted into quite a presentable church. The tiny belfry and large front porch, the windows set high up in the walls: all pointed to the church influence on its designer, and a passer-by would have been easily able to identify it as one of many schools belonging to the ecclesiastical authorities.

It was, of course, impossible to see out of the windows while seated in class, which probably helped one to concentrate on the lessons. The heavy doors, which might have been taken from a church, helped to give a feeling of remoteness from the outside world. These same doors were responsible for many a tear-stained face, and provided the local doctor with a steady income from the treatment of crushed fingers which had been caught in them. From time to time notices were pinned on them, warning boys not to slam the doors, but healthy headstrong boys seldom bother with notices.

---

[23] School transfer was at age 8 plus.

[24] The site of the Boys' School on Watford Road is opposite the end of Bateman Road and is now occupied by flats by the name of 'Magisters Lodge'. Perhaps the name is a reference to 'Neggy' Wilson. The only survivors from his day are a row of fine beech trees against the boundary with the Duke of York Public House (now also replaced by housing), which Frank Paddick probably knew as a beech hedge.

The morning that I left the infants' school, in company with eight or nine other boys, we were marched along the road and straight into our new classroom, where the teacher was awaiting our arrival. We all stood in front of the class while she called our names and entered them in the register. Long association with many small boys had no doubt familiarised her with their ways, for she realised at once that I was in some discomfort and told me to leave the room – she would attend to me after playtime.

She had correctly anticipated my needs, and I hastily left the classroom and ran across the playground to the privy. I had just prepared myself for the purpose of my visit when I was attacked from behind: a pair of huge hands held my shoulders and forced me backwards so that the back of my head was only an inch or so from the floor. While I was being thus roughly handled a loud voice bellowed in my ear, 'Let's see you do it! Let's see you do it!' I was kept in the horizontal position for a few moments, then gradually raised to stand on my feet once more, when I was able to see my tormentor for the first time. He was a huge boy with a shock of unruly ginger hair, his teeth already blackened by smoking. I was later to learn that he was unteachable, and when anything outside the daily round was taking place, or when his teacher could put up with him no longer, he was turned loose in the playground. Meanwhile he kept my arms in a vice-like grip and continued to repeat 'Let's see you do it'.

Finally it penetrated even his dull brain that I had no earthly idea what he was talking about, so, releasing his hold on me he said, 'Here, like this' and sent a stream of urine about three feet over the privy wall. My feeble attempt to emulate this feat he viewed with contempt, and breaking off his demonstration proceeded in the same manner to write his initials on the long slate slab which lined the privy interior, saying, 'Here, have a go at this'. By this time the other boys had been released from school and were rushing into the playground and the privy, and my tormentor found someone else to bully. This was the one and only occasion that I was alone with the ginger-haired gentleman, but not the last that I should test my skill over the privy wall.

This rare accomplishment was considered essential by all the boys, and was freely indulged in. It was no uncommon sight to see six or seven boys of varying ages from eight to fourteen displaying themselves while they vied with each other to send the highest stream over the wall. Many a proud mother would have been horrified to hear the remarks of her innocent little son while testing his skill in this manner. To clear the wall by two or three feet was considered a feat of great prowess.

The headmaster had been trying to stamp out this habit for years, and whenever boys were caught the result was a mass caning, which brought a temporary lull. Occasionally a boy running by would be caught in the spray. This would lead to a letter from his mother; the school would be assembled, and a long lecture delivered on the disgusting habit of 'precipitating dirty water over the wall' and a stern warning given. But only a roof on the privy would have stopped the habit permanently: an open wall to small boys engaged in this function was a challenge which would always prove irresistible.

My new classroom was crowded with bits and pieces of all sorts and sizes. Miss Bray, my new teacher, had reigned in this same room for many years, and was renowned for her teaching and for helping her pupils to collect and construct many things which occurred in the lessons. Any boy who made something which she considered of especial merit had his handicraft hung on the classroom wall. Consequently the room was festooned with Roman helmets, breastplates, swords, spears, sleighs, coracles, kayaks, and many more objects than I can list, even if I could call them all to mind. Many of these had hung there for so many years that their makers were now married men, or fighting on the fields of Flanders.

The window ledges were crowded with shells and stones of varying shapes and sizes. We were well aware of Miss Bray's interest in geological specimens or natural history 'finds', and these we would bring to school and give to her just before lessons began. She, as we hoped, would often become so absorbed in identifying and describing anything handed to her that she would forget the lesson which she should have been taking until well after it should have been in progress.

In this classroom was a large oak desk, rather like a pulpit with three steps, and from this elevated position Miss Bray presided over her pupils.

A good teacher will observe her charges closely, and familiarise herself with them and their ways, but however much she feels that she knows them, there will always be some in the class who have studied her more closely than she has studied them. In our class there were two boys who could imitate Miss Bray's every gesture, and mimic her voice

36

to absolute perfection. She would often leave the classroom for short periods, when either or both of these boys would leave their desks and mount to her pulpit-like one, giving from this exalted position their impersonation of the good lady.

Perhaps Miss Bray had some idea of the performances which took place when she left the room, for she always gave good warning of her return. Her steps could be heard well before she lifted the latch of the door, and she always seemed to hesitate in doing so, so that there was another instant's pause before the door opened.

 It was in this room that I remember my hardest struggles with the pen and ink. The school had long been renowned for the handwriting of its scholars, and the headmaster and his assistants were determined to uphold this reputation. For me, at least, it would have been less difficult had our equipment been in better shape. Pen-nibs, which were of the best and, in the hands of a good pen-man, could help to produce beautiful handwriting, were issued only very sparingly. These same nibs had to be jealously guarded as they were in much demand for paper darts, which were constantly thrown in the classroom whenever the teacher's back was turned. These could be very painful when striking the face or neck – an assault one was expected to bear without so much as a gasp of pain, as the boys considered it very unsporting to let the teacher know that these missiles were hurtling round the room.

Another hazard to good writing lay in the ink wells, which I believe were cleaned and refilled every Friday afternoon in readiness for a fresh start on Monday morning. This was not enough to keep them uncontaminated, however, for some of the boys took a mischievous delight in putting foreign bodies into them. The handiest thing, and often the most satisfying, was blotting paper, for if the ink were getting low this would cause it to practically dry up, while in any case the unwatchful victim, dipping in his pen might well bring it out with a lump of blotting paper attached and make a sorry mess of the sheet on which he was writing. Carbide from bicycle lamps was another very successful addition to any ink well, but here more care was required. A tiny chip would produce a dirty smell under the victim's nose, and sometimes a head of evil-looking bubbles on top of his ink. The slightest miscalculation, however, sent the ink foaming over the desk-top, and

37

brought the unwelcome attention of the teacher – and sometimes of the other boy's parents, for ink-stained clothes caused trouble at home. I have not seen a carbide lantern,[25] such as were normal on bicycles for some time, for many a long day, but the smell – that is one thing no-one familiar with it will forget!

But to me, at least, the greatest bar to good writing was the insistence by the teachers that we must always have two fingers on top of the pen. This was a fetish of either the headmaster or of someone in higher authority, and it was held that one couldn't hope to acquire good handwriting unless one's fingers remained in this position. No matter how good your writing was, hold the pen in any other way and you were in trouble. Teachers would patrol their classes, reprimanding a scholar here, tapping knuckles there, correcting all deviations from the rule. I am afraid that I soon gave up trying to improve my writing and gave the teacher the satisfaction of seeing both fingers on the pen.

About this time, too, someone decreed that ordinary longhand writing was outmoded and old-fashioned: we were all ordered and taught to write script. Parents who complained that their children were being taught only childish printing were solemnly assured that script was the modern form of writing, and would entirely supersede longhand. For the next four or five years children were only allowed to use script, but just before I left school the order was rescinded. We were informed that we

---

[25] Carbide lamps were developed in the 1890s. They were first used for carriage lamps, and were quickly adapted for mining. The lamp has a removable base which would be unscrewed and filled with marble-sized pellets of calcium carbide. A small amount of water was poured into a reservoir in the top part of the lamp. A tap controlled the amount of water which would slowly flow from the reservoir into the carbide chamber below. The water reacted with the carbide to form acetylene gas, which rose to the top of the carbide chamber into a small tube, which led out of the chamber to a burner tip. This could be lit with a flint, and the flame produced was focused by a shiny reflector to give a bright white light, between four and six times brighter than an oil lamp or flame safety lamp. http://www.lindal-in-furness.co.uk/MinersLamps/minerslamps.htm accessed 9 March 2011

might either write the usual longhand or continue to use the script, to which after some years we had become accustomed.

This was the first step towards the abandoning of script: it had probably been discovered that while script was much clearer, it was too slow and laborious for ordinary use. Soon it was taught no longer, but many children of the period left school without having been taught to write in the recognised style.

Pupils at Croxley Boys' School[26]

I wonder how many teachers think (or trouble) to put themselves in the position of their pupils? Literally, I mean, to take a seat among the desks and view their class-room from the other direction. I don't think Miss Bray can ever have done this, or she would have seen what occupied so much of my time, and distracted my attention from the lessons. Or perhaps she had seen it, and with her superior intelligence made more sense of it than I could.

---

[26] This photo is in the collection at Croxley Green library and listed under the heading 'undated photo of ? Croxley Boys' School'. The inscription on the reverse reads 'Vicar Rev. Donnell [Vicar of All Saints' from 1899 to 1913] and Teacher Miss Stamford who later became headmistress of the Girls' School'.

Hanging above the fireplace was a large picture of a shepherd, walking with his crook and surrounded by sheep. Above his head was a scroll almost the width of the picture and with the two ends hanging down on either side of the shepherd. On the scroll was a religious text: something about the shepherd leading his flock to Glory. The trouble for me was that it didn't make sense. Whichever way I read the text it didn't seem right. If I started to read in the top left-hand corner (where I'd been taught to start, and there was a red capital letter there, anyway), continued to the end of the wide scroll, and then worked down first the left-hand 'tail' and then the right it was meaningless. If I read across the top, down the right-hand column and back up the left, it was no better. Wherever I started or finished the text remained incomprehensible.

While I should have been employed in reading, writing or arithmetic, listening to Miss Bray or following her demonstrations on the blackboard, I found myself constantly trying to decipher the message on the picture. Why, I wonder, did I lack the courage to raise my hand and ask Miss Bray to read the word on the picture for me? Over forty years later I was telling an old boy of the school, who had sat in the same classroom some years before me about this, and he confessed that like me, he had spent many hours trying to unravel the message of the scroll. Perhaps the subconscious mind finally rejects anything it finds too perplexing or incomprehensible, for the exact words on the scroll, which I thought indelibly imprinted on my mind, have gone for ever, although I can recall many other words memorised at about the same time.

Unlike many of my class-mates, I could easily memorise poetry or passages from Shakespeare or other writers. But then, many scholars who could only stumble haltingly through any verse given them to learn found no difficulty in committing to memory any of the many verses in circulation with a hint (sometimes more than that) of vulgarity in them. One of the most popular at this time ran:

> Oh, the white cat piddled in the black cat's eye,
> The white cat, said 'Gawd Blimey,
> If you stick your nose up my behind
> You won't be far behind me.

Along the land which led to our village school was a large hawthorn tree some fifteen or twenty feet high. This was draped with thick strands of briony, and boys long before my time had converted it into a slide. You climbed up the trunk of the tree and then out on to the top for the slide down. At times there would be a procession of boys up and down, and the activity was often accompanied by the chanting of

Higher up the mountains,
Greener grows the grass,
I saw a Chinaman
Sliding on his
Ask no questions
Hear no lies
I saw a Chinaman
Doing up his
Flies are a nuisance,
Flies are a pest
I saw a Chinaman
Taking off his vest.

The slide ended, or more correctly began, in the hedge, from which the long tendrils had reached out and enveloped the hawthorn, creating a perfect slide for venturesome boys.

This same briony, daddy-beard, or granny-beard, as it was usually called, was in great demand for smoking. This was indulged in by almost all boys at different times, but I don't recall real tobacco being smoked very often. With cigarettes three-halfpence or twopence for five, substitutes were always being tried: there were too many ways to spend twopence, without wasting it on tobacco. Daddy-beard was the smoker's first choice. One selected a length of the vine which was old and dry, and cut it into pieces about the length of a cigarette. Running through this woody stuff are hundreds of tiny tubes through which air can pass, and the dry vine itself will smoulder for a long time. Thus one lit one end, put the other to one's lips and drew a mouthful of smoke. It was possible to give quite a convincing imitation of smoking a cigarette in this way, but others preferred the pipe.

Clay pipes of all shapes and sizes were easily acquired: they were extremely cheap, and were often given away by publicans and tobacconists. Sometimes we would make our own pipes from a tiny acorn-cup, with any hollow twig or straw for a stem. In these pipes dried leaves were smoked, one boy declaring oak or beech to be the best and another swearing by apple or cherry. Another source of smoking material was blotting paper, which was rolled tight and smoked in the privy or play-ground.

None of these things had the injurious effects that one might have predicted, as they all tasted so vile that they were never inhaled, but rather blown. I think they gave us the satisfaction of knowing that what we were doing was forbidden, and of aping our elders, rather than any pleasure to be derived from smoking.

The school belfry was above the classroom, and the rope dangled in the middle of the room. It was frequently used for swinging on when the teacher was out of the room. There was much competition for the honour of ringing the bell. This was done twice daily, at five to nine in the morning and five to two in the afternoon, and each week the schoolmaster appointed a new boy to this important duty.

The school day began with an inspection in the playground. The boys were lined up with their hands outstretched, palms upwards. The schoolmaster walked down the line once, and then on the word of command all hands were turned over to reveal the backs. Boots or shoes, too, were examined with some thoroughness to make sure they had received their daily polish. If there was any doubt the boy concerned was ordered to 'about turn' and have his heels inspected. 'Neggy' Wilson, our schoolmaster, was very keen on heels, for he knew that any boy who hurriedly cleaned his boots when they were already on his feet was inclined to forget the backs. Hair was inspected, to make sure that it had seen a comb before its owner came to school.

Any boy who didn't measure up to the required standard would be severely reprimanded for being untidy or slovenly, and the persistent offender sent home to clean his boots or correct any other faults.

We were, on the whole, a very prosperous village. Most of our fathers were employed in the paper mill, and in steady employment. It was, however, the day of the big family, and if there was no real poverty, many mothers were hard put to it to keep their children respectable. Respectability was the goal all our mothers strove for, the will-o'-the-wisp they all pursued. Make do and mend was the order of the day, and clothes which survived their first owner were handed down from elder brother or sister to younger. The seats of most boys' trousers had either been patched or would soon need such attention, and it was not without reason that one boy sometimes called after another
Giddy giddy Gout, your shirt's hanging out,
Half-a-yard in and half-a-yard out,

42

Giddy giddy Gout, your shirt's hanging out.

Periodically the local doctor would arrive at school in company with the district nurse, and we would all be weighed and measured, have our teeth and tonsils examined, and our hair inspected. There was much preoccupation with hair at that time, and sometimes the nurse would arrive by herself and make a show of examining all our heads, but on these occasions it was always common knowledge in the school who she was really after, and one of the staff had doubtless warned her where to look.

The greatest fear of all good mothers, and they were about ninety-nine per cent of the total, was that nurse would 'find something' in their children's hair. This would have been a humiliation beyond bearing for these good women, and they made sure it wasn't likely to happen. One had only to scratch one's head in the slightest way and out would come the fine-toothed comb and a sheet of white paper. The suspect head was then subjected to a vigorous combing which almost made it sore. This was the only form of hunting I know in which the hunter devoutly hoped that she wouldn't find something: the only hunt where the huntress gave a sigh of relief when she didn't make a kill.

CHAPTER SIX

Schoolmaster 'Neggy' Wilson

Staff and students of Croxley Boys' School in 1934 at the retirement of H.T. (Neggy) Wilson

In retrospect it seems to me our village was administered by an unofficial committee of four: the schoolmaster, vicar, mill manager and doctor – and what characters they were. I recall calling at the doctor's surgery one morning for some medicine for the old lady who lived next door to me. On knocking at the surgery door the doctor came.

'I've called for Mrs. 'Oward's medicine, sir,' I said.
'Mrs. Who?', replied the doctor.
''Oward, sir.'
He looked at me sternly. 'Say Howard, coward. Give them a full, round sound. You speak the language of Shakespeare, don't mutilate it. Howard, coward. Coward, Howard. Try those for a few minutes.'

44

Revd. Bloiss-Bisshopp, Vicar of All Saints' Croxley Green from 1917 to 1933

Charles Barton-Smith (1854-1929), Manager of Dickinson's Croxley Mill

The doctor retired to his surgery, returning after a few moments with an envelope which he gave me, saying, 'Keep on with the Howards and cowards. Come round for the medicine after school – and give this letter to Mr. Wilson' – our village schoolmaster and known to us all as 'Neggy'.[27]

It was later in the day when Neggy assembled the school and said, 'I have a letter here from Dr. Evans. A letter of great importance: one it pains me to have to read'. The letter complained of our slovenly speech, and implored Neggy to devote more time to teaching us the King's English. I can't remember the exact wording of the letter, but recall that it concluded, 'And finally, Mr. Wilson, I frequently have boys calling at my surgery for <u>sustificates</u>. I do not have <u>sustificates</u>, but I will

---

[27] Henry Thomas Wilson born about 1870 in Kingsgate, near Broadstairs, Kent. He was Headmaster of Croxley Boys' School from 1903 to 1934. In 1911 he lived with two unmarried sisters at 37 New Road. See *Rickmansworth Historian,* 5, pp.75-82 and 8, pp.164-167.

always provide a boy with a certificate should his state of health render it necessary'.

All this may have been pre-arranged by Dr. Evans and Neggy, as perfect English and a good speaking voice were Neggy's pet subjects, and this was probably his way of showing that good speech was not merely a foible of the schoolmaster's, but was of equal importance to the doctor. Always the original approach, as Reg Childs will tell you.

Reg was a boy given to swearing rather more than became one of his tender years, and had been overheard on several occasions by Neggy.

'Childs, I seem to have noticed that you like swearing.'
'Me, sir?' said Reg.
'Yes, you, Childs. Now Childs, there is not a lot wrong with swearing, provided you swear where people don't mind. You like swearing; I can stand it, but there are those who find it most objectionable, and it's those whom we have to consider. I am going to give you, Childs, a chance to enjoy yourself. Fetch your chair.'

Reg having fetched a chair, it was placed in the middle of the play-ground.

'Now Childs,' said Neggy, 'you may have the entire day going through your swear words. Suppose we start with such a one,' said Neggy, mentioning a good round swear word. Reg spent the entire day marooned on his chair in the middle of the play-ground. At intervals Neggy would pop out: 'I can't hear anything,' says he, 'I thought you liked it. Now, try this one. Come along, we'll try it together.'

To swear amongst one's schoolmates is one thing; to swear to your schoolmaster is another, and Reg found the words would just not come, and spent a most unhappy day.

When he came to us at the turn of the century we were a small village with less than a hundred scholars. Now we have a Grammar School, a Secondary Modern school and various other schools – but we haven't a 'Neggy'.

Founder of the Croxley Society and chairman of the cricket club, he would referee a football match or umpire a cricket match with strict impartiality. It was 'Neggy' who levelled and rolled that part of the village green where all our festivities take place.

Should a boy be a cricket enthusiast or a lover of drama, it was 'Neggy' who first took him to Lord's or the Old Vic. A man of great culture, 'he nothing common did, or mean' during a lifetime of service to his fellow men. Who of us will forget his performances as Father Time, leading the King George VI Coronation procession and acting every inch of the way, or his yearly reading of *A Christmas Carol*: his laughter as old Fezziwig and his scowls as Scrooge?

We have erected a memorial seat to 'Neggy' beneath the shade of the Jubilee oak[28], a seat which will endure for centuries – but it will not endure as long as the ideals for which he worked and which he sought so earnestly to spread among his fellow men.

'Neggy's' bench on the Green

---

[28] The tree planted in 1935 to commemorate George V's Silver Jubilee to the north of New Road at its junction with the Green.

CHAPTER SEVEN

The birds (and the bees)

'Yea, the sparrow hath found an house and the swallow a nest for herself, where she may lay her young.'[29] The sparrow twitters from the gutters of the house, while the swallow and swift shrill backwards and forwards down our long village street. The little chaffinch forages for his daily bread where the tradesman's horse has lately paused. The tiny linnet hangs on the wall, and from the narrow confines of his cage forever raises his voice in vain but sweet protest. The great cockerel mounts the barn door and stretches his neck in loud defiance of all his fellows within hearing distance. Well may he challenge and taunt his neighbours, for they will never meet. They too are, like him, lords of a dozen or so backyard hens. Securely caged in their wire netting harems, they merely await the day when they will be pronounced ready for the oven.

Today the wild birds come to the bird table for the household scraps, while fowls are members of some distant battery unit. In my boyhood they were all part of our lives. The backyard chicken pen played an important part in the cottagers' economy, and few were without some. The larger family might have had two or three dozen birds, and the lone widow four or five. Much of the conversation between neighbours concerned the laying powers of White Leghorn and Wyandotte, while the table merits of Buff Orpington and Rhode Island Red were frequently compared. Each year broody hens were watched for and two or three settings of thirteen eggs put down. When the chicks were old enough for the sex to be determined, the cocks and hens were separated; the cocks for fattening and the pullets to take the place of the old hens, which would be killed off when the pullets began to lay. In this way the poultry-keeper secured a constant supply of fresh eggs, and quite a few Sunday dinners in the course of the year.

But if our parents were preoccupied with domestic birds, it was the wild ones which attracted the village boys, and these they pursued without mercy through all seasons of the year. No bird was safe from our attentions except the little robin: there were too many superstitions surrounding him, and he consequently bore a charmed life. Every boy

---

[29] Psalm 84, v. 3 (Authorised version)

could quote instances of a boy who took a robin's egg and then fell out of a tree and broke a leg, or who killed a robin and met some even worse fate.

There was no close season for the birds, for as they changed their seasonal habits, their tormentors would change theirs. There were sieve traps, brick traps, bird lime, ground nets, batfolding nets and catapults. Many people think of the catapult as a harmful toy, but in the hands of an expert it is an extremely powerful weapon. Silent in operation and easily concealed in a pocket, it was much favoured by country men and boys. The effective catapult was no hastily or casually made tool, but a precision job carefully constructed by its owner. Woods and hedges were searched for suitable prongs – sometimes a pair would be found which were not quite perfect, when they would be bound up with string and left to grow into the desired shape. Pebbles were selected with great care – if used at all, for some men had crucibles and a mould, with which they made their own lead missiles. So deadly were these weapons that they could not only kill a small bird, but very easily stun or kill both rabbits and pheasants. It is always cruel to kill or catch wild birds, and fortunately the country youth finds something else to do with his leisure today.

Of all the many methods of catching birds, brick traps and bird lime always seemed the most cruel to me. Bird lime I have seen used to catch goldfinches. In late Autumn on cold days these birds seemed to turn to the thistles on the moor for their food, and large flocks of them could be seen clinging to the thistle-heads and extracting the seed. The ripe thistle-heads would be smeared with bird lime, a thick treacly substance, and the poor unsuspecting birds would get this on their wing feathers and be unable to fly, when the hunters would emerge from behind bush or tree to pick up the helpless creatures. They were then taken home and their feathers cleaned. Happily the birds either saw or smelt the birdlime, for they generally seemed to avoid the prepared thistles. I have seen many attempts to catch goldfinches in this way, but on the whole the catches were few.

Brick traps were designed to catch individual birds, and were made by using three whole bricks and two halves. A small hole was dug in the ground, and two whole bricks placed in it with just enough space between them for the two half-bricks at each end, these being sunk at a lower level than the whole ones. The third whole brick was then delicately balanced on two twigs of wood, and a bait for the bird placed inside the trap. Like bird lime these traps were often not very successful, firstly because the birds were reluctant to venture into the semi-darkness, and secondly because the balance had to be very fine for a small bird to upset it. Sometimes the brick would fall just as the bird was going in or out, crushing and killing it.

 'Dickerdy, dickerdy, dickerdy wren!' This cry would set boys of all ages within hailing distance searching for stones, bricks, sticks or anything which could be thrown, while they hurried to the spot where the tiny wren had been seen. For some unknown reason the wren, which always seemed to be called a 'Jenny' wren elsewhere, was known in our district as a 'dickerdy'. When once the dapper little bird had been sighted, old and young boys surrounded the bush or hedge and threw anything they could lay their hands on. The wren, however, seemed to bear a charmed life – it is much harder to hit a bird in the middle of a bush than most people would suppose. The wren hopped with apparent unconcern from one twig to another, and the missiles which had been hurled with such venom at this inoffensive little creature always managed to hit a bough or get lodged in the bush. I have seen gangs of boys on many occasions attacking the wren, but I cannot recall one being killed. I can, though, remember a boy's face being cut by a piece of slate which had missed the wren and passed straight through the bush.

Eventually the wren would do what it should have done in the first place: fly away. It is the only bird I know that will remain in a bush at the approach of man, and I have always assumed that it was this habit which attracted the attention of the country boy. I have since learned that 'hunting the wren' is an age old custom all over the British Isles, and in many places gangs of men went out to hunt the wren every St. Stephen's Day[30]. At Kirkmaiden[31] it was a New Year custom to catch a wren, tie ribbons to it, and set it free, while in Ireland bands of youths would go through the lanes on St. Stephen's Day dressed in straw, with blackened faces and carrying a captive wren on the end of a staff.

The most lucrative and effective method for the bird-catcher is the ground net, and this was used mainly by men who sold their catch in

---

[30] St Stephen's Day is 26 December
[31] Kirkmaiden is a small village in Galloway.

quantity to bird-fanciers. It was a winter pursuit, and in our neighbourhood linnets and goldfinches were the target. In winter-time they gather in flocks, when they are much more vulnerable to the bird catcher. These bird nets were some ten or twelve yards square and were spread flat upon the ground, where they were secured by four iron pins. The two sides of each net, forming flaps, were left free, and threaded through them was the pull-line. On the middle of the net stands a fine wire cage containing the call bird, carefully chosen for its singing powers. Dotted round about the cage are several stuffed birds and scattered over the net is bird-seed. The bird-catcher will then run his pull-line some fifty or sixty feet, to a position behind a hedge or tree if possible – otherwise he will lay flat on the ground.

The call-bird, which has been kept covered up, seeing daylight for the first time that day, will generally start to sing, and with luck some of the wild birds both seeing and hearing it will be attracted to the spot. The bird-catcher will wait until he considers he has enough birds in the net and then jerk the pull-line, when the two flaps will fly over and enclose both wild birds and cage. On good days in a good spot it was not uncommon to catch two or three dozen birds at one pull.

But the greatest adventure of all was batfolding (and why it should be called batfolding I do not know, for never once have I heard of a bat being caught in the batfolders' nets). A batfolding gang generally consisted of a dozen or so men and boys, and during my boyhood there were two or three rival gangs operating in our village. To make a batfolding net two long poles, some twelve or fourteen feet in length, are needed, usually of ash. These poles are then bent to form an arch and hinged in the middle with leather. The 'archway' is then covered with netting, the bottom of the net being folded some two or three feet back up the poles to form a pocket. The bottoms of the poles, below the netting, form the handles which the netsman holds. Three or four other long poles are needed for the beaters.

When the long summer days had passed and the falling leaves heralded the approach of winter the village lads repaired old nets or made new ones, which would provide them with much of their excitement from October to February. Batfolding was the most thrilling, exciting and adventurous 'sport' indulged in by the village men and boys. It had everything: it gave us the thrills of the foxhunter with the added fears and emotions of the poacher, for we were both hunters and hunted.

There were mixed feelings among the local farmers – we were welcomed by some and suspected by others.

No weather seemed to deter the batfolding gangs: we went out on wet nights, frosty nights and snowy nights. We stumbled across ploughed fields, fell in the deep ruts of country lanes and were bogged down in the mud round farm-yard gates. Over stiles and through gaps in hedges we went, with hands and knees scratched by thorn and bramble, clothing torn by barbed wire. We traipsed over meadowland, moorland and parkland; forced our way through woods and thickets; ventured within yards of lordly mansions, and disturbed the inhabitants of remote country cottages. We hid under hedges when we fancied we were being followed, and helped ourselves to a supper of raw swede when it was to be had, while resting and listening to the bleating of the distant sheep and the far-off barking of the dog fox.

Rousebarn Lane

Most of our batfolding was done along the hedgerows or the edges of woods, for if one penetrated deeper into the woods there was insufficient room to operate the nets. Generally two or three beaters would go on one side of the hedge while the rest of the gang with their nets took up positions on the other. Beating would begin, and the birds scared from their roosts flew towards the netsmen. Mostly the birds would fly blindly into the nets, for they seldom took wing until the spot where they had settled for the night was being beaten. Sometimes a keen-eyed and agile netsman, seeing a bird, would jump and literally pluck it from the night sky.

When the bird or birds had been caught, the net was lowered to the ground and all the gang pounced on it to extricate the struggling birds. While the beaters called over the hedge to know how many and what kind of birds had been caught, the others feverishly struck matches or tried to identify them by the glimmer of the small oil-lamp which was part of the recognised equipment, for not only did batfolding provide the thrills of both hunter and poacher, it was akin to angling in that one did not know what the catch was until it was in the hand

Once identified the bird was placed in a bag, unless it happened to be the luckless sparrow, in which case it was promptly killed. The dead sparrows were kept in another bag as evidence, for it was keeping down the sparrow population which gained us the approval of some of the farmers.

Waterdell Spring

Many of the houses in the village were ivy-clad or covered in creeper, and these yielded a rich harvest in sparrows. Like the farmers some householders welcomed us, regarding the sparrows as a nuisance, and others refused us permission to 'try the ivy'.

Batfolding, like angling, could be a very chancy pastime. Some nights the birds would be caught in hundreds, others one could go for miles without, in the batfolders' words, 'seeing so much as a feather': it depended upon how high or low the birds had decided to roost. But, good nights or bad nights, we always pressed on: if it was a good night it was stupid to go home while the luck was in, and if it was a bad night it couldn't last – luck was bound to change. Over the hills and down in the vales while the trees stood out stark and bare and the moon raced across the sky; floundering in ditches and scrambling up banks when one could barely see a yard in front: it was all one to the batfolders.

It was the excitement of the chase rather than the final reward which fired us, for it was a mixed bag we sorted out when the night's hunt was over: linnets, all the finch family, the hastily released robin, thrushes and blackbirds. How we hated the blackbird, and how dearly he sold his freedom! No light was needed to identify him – the moment the beaters hit the hedge he began to protest. If he flew into the net he could be speedily silenced, but if he was too wary and escaped he set up a fearful din, and flew in terror squawking his fears along the hedges, while we listened to his cries dying away and cursed him for alerting every bird within a mile radius. Strangely enough, he soon adapted himself to captivity – for to cage them was the reason for this constant assault on the wild birds.

The demand for birds created a great need for cages, and these were many and varied, ranging from the tiny one which housed the linnet to the large one where the proud thrush fretted his short life away. Most cottage homes had a bird, and apart from the canary they were all native wild birds. They hung in the window during the cold days of winter, and hung on the back wall through the warm summer months. The travelling tinker had one swinging in his caravan door, and on the cabin-tops of the great barges passing up and down the canal could be seen almost every species of bird as one paused to watch during the Sunday afternoon stroll. Not only were birds in demand as songsters: the stuffed bird, too, was a popular household ornament. There were glass cases so large that they contained half-a-dozen pheasants or partridges, or a wide sample of our wild birds, and there were tiny cases with a solitary woodpecker or kingfisher.

For caging the little linnet was immensely popular. It and the nightingale were considered the best songsters of all our native birds. Rivalling them in popularity was the goldfinch, for apart from its great beauty it is one of the longest-lived of cage birds. This finch was also prized because of all wild birds it most readily pairs with the canary. The offspring, known as 'mules', frequently combine the singing powers of the canary with the beauty of the goldfinch. The green-finch too would pair with the canary, but neither that nor the more common chaffinch was so highly valued.

Bullfinches were very rare in our part of the country, but their nests were occasionally found in the hazel copses. These nests were closely watched, and when the young birds were almost fully-fledged a net was placed round the nest and the parents would continue to feed the youngsters through it. Twice-daily visits would have to be made to these nests, for once the young bullfinches became restive at this enforced confinement their fluttering efforts to free themselves would attract unwelcome predators, or they could strangle themselves in the netting. This was also a very common method of obtaining blackbirds and thrushes.

Today the budgerigar seems to hold pride of place among pet birds, largely due to its readiness to learn to talk, but many of our own birds can compare with it in beauty and surpass it as songsters. The bullfinch, too, can be taught to pipe, and the starling, one of our most despised birds today, will learn to talk. Fifty years ago it was the most popular bird for stuffing, but now this speckled beauty, regarded by so many as a pest for its habit of congregating on buildings, goes unappreciated.

These, then, were the birds which filled our lives – what of the bees?

There are, I believe, many kinds of bees. There was the bee which lived in a hole in the wall and seemed to spend her days in sawing off pieces of leaves and carrying them into her hideout. Best-known of all there is the honey-bee, beautifully housed in her man-made hive, but there were only two kinds of bees which interested us boys and helped to fill our days. These were the large humble or bumble bees, known to

55

us by their most distinguishing feature as white bums and red bums. The white bums were most difficult to obtain as they made their nests in banks whence they had to be dug out, or in trees from which they had to be chopped or sawn to obtain the honeycomb without which they could not be persuaded to return to a new home.

Greater favourites were the red bums, which made their homes in balls of moss about the size of tennis balls. These could be found in the hedgerows, in long grass, or in patches of stinging nettles, and could swiftly be lifted bodily into a box or tin, when they were taken home in triumph. They had no value except the boyish one of having something of one's own, and great was our delight when we succeeded in making them return to their new homes.

But these bees were seasonal: they belonged to the long summer days and the great outdoors. There was at this time, however, another 'bee' which greatly preoccupied our elders. It did not spend its life buzzing from flower to flower; it neither flew nor stung; it passed its life on the mantel-shelf, confined within the narrow limits of an empty beer bottle. This was the peculiar yeast-like substance known as 'bees'[32], the makers of bee wine. They were kept in bottles of water and fed on sugar. Early in the century no cottage was complete without a few bottles on shelf or dresser.

It was fascinating to watch these 'living snow flakes' going up and down on their never-ending journey. I think they must have varied their activities according to temperature changes, for certainly some days their movements were sluggish, while at other times they were more rapid, when they were said to be 'working very hard'. The bees were frequently talked about, and like real bees were forever increasing in numbers. When the bottles became too crowded they were divided between more bottles or given away: to increase one's stock was a very easy matter. The actual wine was obtained by straining the contents of the bottle through muslin and re-bottling without the bees, which were promptly replaced in fresh water and the whole cycle repeated.

---

[32] 'A lump of a yeast (*Saccharomyces pyriformis*) intermittently rising and releasing bubbles in brew;—usually in *pl.*' Oxford English Dictionary www.oed.com/view/Entry/16941?rskey=fTKRt9&result=1#eid24589278 accessed 14 Feb 2011.

There were many recipes for the finished wine, and bottles were often swapped between neighbours and compared for strength, flavour and colour much as one might discuss a favourite port or beer. The death sentence of the 'bees' was, I believe, passed by the doctors, who considered the wine injurious to health in some way or other, I do not recall how. Certainly they disappeared from our homes, never to be seen again.

CHAPTER EIGHT

An expedition to Rickmansworth

Catapult elastic could neither be made nor grown, and to obtain it we would have to journey to Rickmansworth, or Ricky to us locals. Before we could go we had to obtain some money, and as money neither grows nor flies, it had to be worked for. The steadiest income was earned by taking mill dinners, for with the mill working twelve-hour shifts, and no canteen, the men's dinners were taken to the mill in wicker baskets. The payment for this was sixpence a week per dinner, so if one were big enough to carry two baskets, and fortunate enough to have two patrons, a regular shilling a week could be earned.

One had to be both quick and careful at this job: quick because the men liked their dinners hot (and also because one had to get back to school); careful because each dinner was in two separate basins, and if carried at all lop-sided the sweet and the meat and veg. might end up together in the basket.

There were many other ways of making a few coppers, but they were mostly seasonal. In any event, having obtained our money from one source or another, we were able to make our journey.

Croxley Great Barn

58

It seems strange on looking back that the two miles between us and Rickmansworth seemed such a long way in those days. Those unfamiliar with the by-ways would doubtless keep to the main road, but we boys chose the less frequented paths. Through Wood Shott and down by Croxley Hall Farm, where we would pause to peep into our great Tithe Barn – the second largest in England. Five hundred years old, it has sheltered both Royalist and Roundhead in the past. When last I saw it two carts and a tractor were its only occupants, if you except a chicken which scratched in the loose straw on the floor. We used to call the barn 'Wolsey's Slaughterhouse', perhaps because the great Cardinal's sometime home of Moor Park[33] lay only just across the valley.

From the barn the path led on by Caravan (and where *that* name came from I cannot tell), where the footbridge crosses the chuckling River Chess, on its way to keep its never-ending tryst with its sisters the Colne and the Gade in many-watered Rickmansworth. On beside the railway then, where neat dark-red engines went briskly past with their trains of smartly varnished coaches, carrying the worthies of Rickmansworth to London and back, or the Londoner for a quiet day in the Chess Valley.

Then the path led back into the main road, at the beginning of Ricky's High Street, with the old brewery on both sides. Here the watchman still 'called the hours' and the great dray horses champed in the stables or clattered through the cobbled brewery yard. A few more yards and we were passing the home of the Taylor brothers, whose plumbers' sign, standing on a little shelf some ten feet above the pavement, was a statue of *a naked boy*. Yes, a naked boy, in an age of prudery when the very legs of beds and wash-stands wore valances to hide their nakedness. Nakedness generally was considered very nasty.

This boy had a coil of lead pipe hung around his neck and over one shoulder, and we would give him a sly glance in passing, feeling that it would have been more becoming had he worn it elsewhere. The sign

---

[33] Cardinal Wolsey lived at the More, *not* at Moor Park. References:
Heather Falvey, 'The More: Archbishop George Neville's palace in Rickmansworth, Hertfordshire', *The Ricardian*, ix, 118 (Sept 1992) pp. 290-302
Heather Falvey, 'The More: Rickmansworth's Lost Palace', *Hertfordshire's Past,* 34 (Spring 1993), pp.2-16
Heather Falvey, 'The More revisited', *The Ricardian*, xviii (2008), pp.92-99

had long been viewed with mixed feelings by the good townspeople of Rickmansworth, and their doubts were intensified upon the arrival of the double-decker bus. The double-deckers were without tops, and many who could tolerate a naked child when seeing him from street level felt the case to be very different when seated on the top deck of a bus and, so to speak, eye to eye with him.

The Rickmansworth of fifty years ago must surely have been one of the country's most quaint and picturesque small towns, with its many and infinitely gabled roofs, and shop fronts which overflowed on to the pavements, pushing the pedestrian into the road (happily not very crowded in those days). The three rivers which travelled many miles to meet here seemed to honeycomb the town. They meandered along the streets, disappeared into gardens and reappeared under tiny bridges, playing, it seemed, a never-ending game of hide and seek. The children caught their tiddlers within sight of their homes, and paddled within sound of their mothers' voices.

Church Street, Rickmansworth about 1900

The High Street was thronged with many characters, some of whom seemed to have been left from a bygone age. One old gentleman frequently to be seen wore knee breeches, silk stockings, and silver-

60

buckled shoes. Many old trades were still followed; there were saddlers' shops, and a taxidermist's, and many wares were displayed on the pavements or hung outside the shop windows.

Many of the cottage front doors were of the stable type, divided into top and bottom halves, and the old folk would leave the top half open and lean out to watch the passing traffic or gossip with a passer-by. This kind of door is quite common in America, and it is tempting to think that they were first introduced there by Rickmansworth men, for William Penn, the founder of Pennsylvania, lived in this very High Street when he was first married.

But our business was in Church Street, at the shop of an old lady disrespectfully known as Ma Wence. This was a shop to delight schoolboys; crammed full of fishing tackle and other boyhood needs. It was here that we bought our Skylark Warblers – a kind of tin whistle with a long handle protruding from one end. By working the handle up and down one could vary the notes, which were supposed to resemble a skylark's song, and were guaranteed to bring a lovesick skylark to the player's hand, under the impression that he was flying to his mate.

This little shop was a Mecca for boys from the neighbouring villages of Croxley Green, Sarratt, and Chorleywood. We had come to buy elastic for our catapults. Now, Ma Wence had certainly sold some hundreds of yards of elastic for catapults, but it was still necessary to keep up the pretence that it was required for some other purpose. She always asked what one needed elastic for, and the expected answer was, 'For a model boat', or 'For an aeroplane'. Anything, in fact, except 'For a catapult'. Admit the truth and your journey was in vain, for you came away empty-handed.

We had no scruples about calming Ma Wence's conscience, and with our purchase made turned our faces towards Croxley Green and home, towards stronger and better catapults and a new and (may we be forgiven) a fiercer assault on the birds.

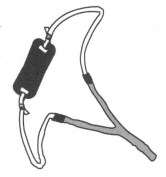

CHAPTER NINE

Sly hogs

'Dear Mother, sell the pig and buy me out' was an expression still frequently used in the village in my boyhood. It had, I assume, come down from the days when the pig would be the only valuable possession of the cottager: the only thing that could be sold to raise sufficient to buy a homesick son out of the Army. If it ever had been a serious saying it had ceased to be so in my time, and was used half humorously when one seemed cornered, and affairs so tangled that there seemed no way out.

The saying may have belonged to the past, but the pig was very much part of the present. There were many keepers of pigs, varying from the farmer or smallholder who kept several score to the man or woman who kept one  in the back garden, for at that time there were no restrictions as to where a pig might be kept. There were two or three backyard keepers within throwing distance of my home, and several more within easy smelling range.

There were those who objected to the smell of the backyard pigs, but few who were not prepared to have their piece of pork when the day came to call in the butcher. Perhaps they felt entitled to their joints of meat, for many of them had contributed to the pig's fattening by saving the household scraps. The pig pail or swill bucket stood outside the backhouse door, and into it the housewife threw anything edible: stale bread, scrapings from dinner plates, tops of all root vegetables, apple rinds and potato peelings. It was probably this custom which inspired the rhyme –

> *Dearly beloved brethren, isn't it a sin,*
> *When you peel a tater to throw away the skin?*
> *For the skin feeds the pigs, and the pig feeds us -*
> *Dearly beloved brethren, is it not thus?*

The swill bucket was emptied each morning by the pig-keeper or his wife.

The poor animal, after several months in the backyard sty, seemed almost part of the family. Fortunately he was unconscious of his limbs and body having already been spoken for and allocated among the neighbours. It was said of the pig that you could use every part of him but his squeak, and I think this must have been true, for I cannot remember any waste.

Somehow we small boys always seemed to learn when the butcher had arranged to call, and contrived to be present. Much as we sympathised with the poor pig, we took up vantage positions to watch his demise, and frequently chanted the following parody of the well-known hymn –

> *There is a happy land, far, far away.*
> *Where little piggies run, three times a day.*
> *Oh! How they squeal and run.*
> *When they hear the butcher come.*
> *Cut three slices off their bum, three times a day.*

I have often watched the butcher slaughtering a neighbour's pig, and seen the animal thrown on to a truss of straw for sizing. In addition to the usual cuts or joints the flare was rendered down to make lard, and the remains, known as crinklings or cracklings, were also eaten. The lard was delicious, and they used to say 'you could eat it until you were hungry'. The pig's entrails were washed out by connecting to the kitchen tap, and these chitterlings were in much demand.

Of all the local pig breeders old Joe Dabbs was the leading man. Joe's father had been a farmer of some importance in the neighbourhood, but in middle life had reduced his considerable acreage to some fifteen or twenty and had specialised in pig breeding, which he did with great success. His piggeries were without equal throughout the county, where he enjoyed a wide and well-earned reputation. On the death of his father Joe inherited the farm, the row of cottages where he lived, a few thousand pounds, and the prefix 'old', for until his father's departure he had always been 'young' Joe Dabbs.

Joe was well qualified to follow in his father's footsteps, having been well schooled by the old man in the art of pig keeping. Most of the villagers had a word for Joe – some said he was tight, others close, mean, near or selfish. Joe himself maintained that he was merely careful. His invariable reply when taxed with this meanness was, 'To them that asks I don't give to, and them that don't ask, I know they don't want'. The reputation suited Joe very well.

On succeeding to his inheritance some thirty years before Joe had promptly married Martha, who was remarkable for one thing only: her extreme reticence. Martha seldom spoke unless spoken to, and conserved her words as carefully as her husband did his cash. The union had been blessed with one daughter now in her middle twenties – Pretty Lizzie Dabbs. Lizzie had been a very beautiful baby at birth, and old Joe, contemplating his offspring for the first time had promptly called her 'Pretty Lizzie'. Alas! Poor Lizzie's reign of beauty had been all too brief. With each succeeding year she grew plainer and plainer, and by the time she reached womanhood she was anything but pretty. Perhaps Lizzie was well aware that her beauty was a thing of the past. Certainly all the villagers were, and only old Joe seemed to be obstinately blind. To him she remained Pretty Lizzie, the apple of his eye.

The cattle market in the neighbouring town of Watford was held twice a week, and Joe generally managed to be present on both days, for it was here that he transacted much of his business. Some days he would be buying pigs and sometimes selling – not infrequently both. Tuesday was the day Joe did most of his business, and on this day he preferred to be alone. Most Tuesdays Joe would spend the morning in the market attending to any pigs he had for sale or looking round for any that he might be tempted to bid for. About midday, in company with a few fellow farmers, butchers and dealers, he would adjourn to the King's Head, a public house adjacent to the market, which remained open all day on market days. Tuesday afternoons in the King's Head were the highlights of Joe's life. There, after a few tongue-loosening pints of beer Joe and his cronies swapped yarns, told tales, and put the final seal on many a deal.

Only on very rare occasions and for some special purpose did Martha accompany Joe to the mid-week market. Saturday was her day. It was a great day in the Dabbs household. Joe would rise early and harness the pony to the little trap which he kept in the yard at the back of his cottage. Joe was proud of his pony and trap, and they were as well-known in the village and the nearby town as Joe himself. For many years Lizzie had accompanied her parents to the Saturday market, and

64

while her father attended to his affairs Lizzie and her mother would go round the market and town making enough purchases to last the week.

Watford Market

Old Joe, seated at his early breakfast one Tuesday morning, was astonished when Martha quietly remarked 'I think I will come with you today'. This was unheard of. Always Martha's visits to market had been arranged overnight, and Joe could not recall her making up her mind at so short notice before. All his efforts to dissuade her seemed only to increase her determination. Martha, usually subservient to Joe's every wish, was in a defiant mood this fine October morning. Her insistence was even more surprising as Lizzie had spent a disturbed night, but Martha had already been next door to Emma Smith and obtained her promise to look after Lizzie.

Emma Smith was a widow, and her services were in much demand. Not only did she always manage to be 'in at the death', but was on hand whenever a new baby arrived. She lived by attending the needs of others in all stages of life's journey.

Joe, for once overruled by Martha, grumblingly prepared the pony and trap, and soon both he and Martha were on their way. Hardly

65

had the pony's hoof-beats died away when Lizzie, under the watchful eye of Emma Smith, began to moan and twist and turn on her bed, and in answer to Emma's questions kept repeating, 'I think I've had something that don't agree with me.'

Emma tried everything she could think of to relieve Lizzie, including putting hot-water bottles in the bed, but despite her attentions Lizzie's cries grew louder and louder. Emma, ignoring Lizzie's constant reiterations of 'I've only had something that don't agree with me', and her pleadings not to do so, decided to send for the doctor. A small boy was pressed into service with the promise of a penny reward, and the doctor was soon on his way to the Dabbs house.

Doctor Thomas Evans was, as his name implies, a Welshman. He had settled in the village many years before and was regarded with affection by most of the villagers. He was a dedicated man: dedicated to the relief of pain. He intensely disliked ill-health and was untiring in his attention to any of his patients he thought deserving. He was, however, intolerant of anyone he felt did not help themselves. He loathed tobacco, and had anticipated medical ideas of the effect of smoking on the lungs by more than half a century. His first injunction to his smoking patients was 'Give it up!' He was a deeply religious man, and when his medicines failed he would not despair, but tell his patient to 'Trust in God.'

Cleanliness, too, was almost a religion with him: cleanliness without and cleanliness within. The latter led him to prescribe large doses of castor oil and liquorice powder, remarking, 'We must keep the inside clean, we must keep the bowels open.' The ways and unvarying instructions of the doctor were well known to all, and many referred to him as 'Trust-in-God-and-keep-your-bowels-open-Evans'. One of these was old Joe Dabbs.

Joe, like all men who enjoyed good health, had little time for doctors. From time to time, however, Martha would call in the doctor to Lizzie or herself when he was needed. Joe on these occasions would invariably remark 'You might just as well fan your belly with a stick of rhubarb or smack your arse with a wet lettuce as send for him'. However, he always treated the Doctor with respect, and paid his bills promptly.

Doctor Evans was familiar with the Dabbs house. He entered the bedroom where he had delivered Lizzie – the very room where she now writhed and moaned – and lifting her hand to take her pulse said, 'Now, what's the trouble with you, young lady?' Lizzie momentarily ceased her moaning, gazed mournfully at the doctor and said, 'I must have had something that don't agree with me, sir'. A look of astonishment crossed the doctor's face, and turning back the bedclothes he said, 'Indeed you have, and you know what. You are going to have a baby.' Now Lizzie's lamentations grew louder, and while she cried 'Oh, no, no, no!', the doctor replied 'Oh, yes, yes, yes!'

On one of her visits to the town Lizzie had purchased some undergarments – well, a modern girl would think them cumbersome but for their period they were considered daring and immodest. Lizzie, usually a tidy girl, had forgotten in her distress to put them away, and they now hung over the brass knob of the bedstead, where they caught the doctor's eye. By now in a flaming temper at finding his patient's condition and the total unpreparedness for such an event, he made a great bound for Lizzie's underwear and brandished them aloft with a 'Who do these belong to?'

'Me, Sir.'
'And what do you call them?'
'Kn – kn – knickers', came the faltering reply from the bed.

'Knickers, knickers! They're the cause of your trouble – prancing around in things like these', and with a mighty wrench the doctor tore the offending garments in half, threw them to the floor and kicked them under the bed.

The good doctor, with the help of Emma Smith, soon improvised arrangements for the newcomer's reception, and long before the unsuspecting Joe had called for his first pint in the King's Head he had become a grandfather.

Old Joe had spent a very pleasant day at the market. Business had been good, the beer equally so, and best of all, Martha had been most unobtrusive, spending most of the day quietly shopping or patiently sitting in the little pony trap. It was with a satisfied and contented mind that Joe removed the little pony's nosebag, stepped up into the trap, and with a 'Gee up' set off briskly for home.

Emma Smith had, on the whole, always been treated well and generously by the Dabbs family, but, a natural gossip, she awaited with relish the return of Lizzie's parents, bursting to tell them the news and witness their discomfiture. Soon the sound of the pony heralded the arrival of Mr and Mrs Dabbs, and laden with baskets and parcels of Martha's shopping they entered the house, where Joe's very first words were, 'How's Lizzie?' This was Emma's moment of triumph, and licking her dry lips in an effort to quell her mounting excitement she replied as calmly as possible, 'She's much better now she's had a baby'.

The full significance of Emma's reply was at first not comprehended by Joe, and he said casually, 'She's had a what?' 'A baby', retorted Emma. It now dawned on Joe just what Emma had said, and her manner assured him that it was all too true. 'A baby? She can't have', he screamed, and turning to Martha, who had remained silent, 'There you are, I didn't want you to come to market today'.

Joe Dabbs had known all about babies from early childhood – it hadn't been necessary to teach him about the 'birds and the bees'. Close association with his father's business from the time that he could toddle had taught him all the workings of nature. He was always unconcerned when any unmarried girl in the village gave birth to a child, generally remarking, 'Ah, boys will be boys'. Only the previous week, when Martha had mentioned the condition of a girl well known to them both, he had laconically replied, 'Ah yes, you always get plenty of that after a dry summer'. But now the philosophy that sustained him for other people's trouble seemed to desert him for his own, and he began to rant and rave. 'I can't understand it. She's never been with anybody. She never goes out. It *can't* be true!'

Emma Smith, who had been quietly preparing to leave, replied, 'Well you know what you always say, Mr Dabbs: it's the sly hog as drinks the most wash'.

68

CHAPTER TEN

Wayfarers[34]

The village lay on the path between two Unions or Workhouses, and twice daily the sorry stream of tramps could be seen passing through on their way to a night's shelter. The nearer of these Unions to us was some mile and a half away in Rickmansworth, and there each morning at around eight o'clock these wanderers were discharged from the casual ward, and on the outward journey would reach Croxley Green quite quickly, if such a term can be applied to the shambling gait of these 'gentlemen of the road'.

They were all released together, after having performed their morning stint of wood chopping, or whatever other task had been imposed by authority in return for their night's lodging. They were more conspicuous on the outward journey: more inclined to amble along in twos and threes. Intent on getting well on the way towards their next casual ward, they had no time to knock at the doors to beg, and only the opportunist would stop anyone in the road for a pinch of tobacco or a match.

Known as tramps, vagrants, knights or gentlemen of the road, and to small boys as milestone inspectors, most of them shuffled along with bowed heads as they searched the gutters and pavements for cigarette ends. There were few women members of this motley crowd – the odd couple, man and woman tramping together, and occasionally a woman by herself.

In the middle of the afternoon they began to arrive in the village from the other direction, with little more than a mile to go. They were moving even slower than the morning contingent, as these had walked some ten miles, and were more ready to sit, resting and enjoy any food or drink they might have come by in the day's march. Now, keeping a wary eye open for the village policeman they would knock on doors to beg. It seemed almost an unwritten law that they asked each householder for only one item of their tea. They each carried a tin can with a wire handle, and the can was invariably clean, having been burnished with sand and water in some convenient stream. If the can

---

[34] Published in *Rickmansworth Historian* 16 pp.403-411

was empty they asked for a pinch of tea; if it already contained tea begged from a previous house, then they required a little sugar or milk, and if tea, sugar and milk were already in the can, they needed hot water. Even in this case they often depended on the generosity of the last housewife visited, for sometimes the tea and sugar were so meagre that only the weakest of tea would be brewed, and a kind-hearted housewife would add a little of both tea and sugar to make a good drop of tea, for few men like very weak tea.

At other times tramps would request a piece of bread, knowing that few women would give them just plain bread, but also anything else they happened to have in the house. Most appreciated was meat or bacon, and least appreciated by these wanderers of the highways and by-ways was cheese. This was a regulation issue in all casual wards, and they needed a change of diet.

When they had begged enough food and drink they would find a secluded spot for a meal, the last of the day, before presenting themselves at the Union door for admittance. Their preparations were simple: if the weather happened to be very cold they would light a tiny fire and sit right over it, but generally they dispensed with this luxury. Their most pressing need was to take their boots off.

Watford Union Workhouse, Vicarage Road

Poorly clad as they invariably were, their boots were the poorest part of their dress. Patched, cracked and broken, sometimes with slits in them to ease corns or bunions, they seemed always in need of repair, and their owners could often be seen trying to patch, sew or hammer them. Tied up with string, few of these boots could have been waterproof, and they must have caused considerable discomfort to these poor downtrodden unfortunates.

When these vagrants came to the door of my home I always tried to listen to their conversation. I loved to hear the stories of the more communicative ones. The majority of these travellers were tramps pure and simple: to move from one casual ward to another was their way of life, and most of them desired no other. Many had their regular rounds and reappeared every few months. Work was something they did not take very kindly to, and they had no intention of doing any.

Most interesting by far were the seasonal workers. Sometimes they stayed in casual wards, sometimes in barns, sheds or stables where they happened to be employed at the time, and at other times again they slept under hedgerows or behind hayricks according to the season of the year. The hardened habitual tramp was usually dour, taciturn, reluctant to engage in conversation. He was eager to take what was given him and depart – he was always conscious of the policeman's possible intervention. The seasonal worker was a more cheerful, merry sort of chap. The ups and downs of his way of life had made him something of a philosopher. When kindly received and generously treated he would unburden himself and tell you his life story. Often he would have led the normal domestic life of the day until some change in his circumstances had forced him to adopt his present way of life. The death of a wife, ejection from a tied cottage, failure to live happily with relations: any of these and many others were among the reasons they gave for taking to the road.

With others it was the call of the great gay road, the restless urge to be for ever moving on, a desire for fresh places and for new faces: the impossibility of following a settled way of life. They were wise in the ways of the countryside, and could talk of far away counties and distant towns, of farms in Leicestershire and hop fields in Kent. The seasonal worker followed the planting and harvesting of crops: bean and pea picking in one county, strawberry picking and potato lifting in others. Many of them had regular rounds, and had been employed by the same farmers for many years.

71

Intermingled with these casual labourers was the odd tradesman – mason, carpenter or hurdle-maker. One of these, an itinerant blacksmith, was known by name to my father, having become friendly with him many years before when employed at a local forge. He appeared in the autumn of most years. He was the only member of the travelling fraternity I ever remember being invited into my home. Arriving at the tramp time, about four in the afternoon, he stayed to tea, but refused to sit at the table with the family. He was full of amusing stories and we immensely enjoyed listening to them.

A superb tradesman, the smith could have settled at any one of hundreds of forges in a dozen counties. Any blacksmith who had employed him once was ready to do so again. He seldom remained in the same place more than a few days, however, although he was said to work very hard during this time. Suddenly he would announce his intention of departing, when no amount of pleading or inducement to stay could change his mind. We had several examples of his work which he had made for my father at different times: a pair of pincers (he was considered an expert at pincer-making), a soldering iron, and a branding iron which he had made for burning my father's name into the wooden handles of his tools.

After tea father and the smith would both adjourn to the local public house, where the visitor would be a welcome and enlivening addition to the tap-room company. Father returned at closing-time, but the blacksmith wasn't with him – he had found a night's lodging elsewhere, probably in the stable loft at the pub, where he was always warmly welcomed. It would be at least twelve months before we saw him again. After being a regular caller for several years, his visits ceased and we never heard of him again.

Half a century ago the streets of our towns were thronged with hundreds of diverse characters of all types, their class and occupation being reflected in their mode of dress. The village street, if less crowded, mirrored the same pageant of the time. Hours of work were longer than today, but despite this, men appeared to have more time to spare, and each street corner had its knot of them involved in desultory conversation. The public house wall or seat accommodated a few more who seemed to lack the necessary latch-lifter.

Increased prosperity and the mass-production of clothing produced a greater uniformity of appearance, and a man's trade or occupation is not often obvious from his style of dress, but then one could almost always tell a man's job from his way of dressing – except on Sundays. The navvy had his corduroys tied just below the knee with a little wooden scraper (used to clean his shovel) tucked into the cord. The distinctive aprons of many men proclaimed their callings: the butcher with his blue and white striped one; the brewer's drayman with his heavy leather one, while the white one of the carpenter contrasted with the green baize of the gardener.

There was little provision then for the mill worker to wash and change at work, and many left the mill with the marks of their jobs visible. The stoker who fed the boilers came home still begrimed with coal dust, and the lime and bleach workers both advertised their jobs not only by their looks, but also by their smell.

"Early Morning"
The Lock, Rickmansworth.

No sooner had the narrow boats and barges moored at the paper mill than the bargees' wives made their way into the village to replenish their larders. A race apart were these women, who seemed never to speak to anyone but their fellow-bargees, and dressed in dark clothes, with wide skirts which reached down to their ankles, meeting the long black button-boots which they always wore. With the wide belt at their waist in which they carried the windlass used for releasing the water through the canal lock gates and sluices, there was little likelihood of their being mistaken for anything other than they were. Followed by the

73

half-dozen children who seemed inseparable from each of them, they were good cash customers at the village general store. With few of the household expenses of other working women, a good proportion of their income was spent on food. They lived well, and their large hessian bags always bulged to overflowing on their return to the canal boats.

Somehow every village managed to have its assortment of misfits and oddities. It was an unusual village that couldn't muster a couple of peg-leg gents, one or two hook-armed unfortunates, and a few forced by deafness to resort to the ear-trumpet, and ours was no exception. Fair game to many small boys and hobbledehoys, who seemed to regard it as their mission in life to taunt, hurt and exasperate the afflicted.

Most conspicuous of all on the village street was the 'horsy' man, whose calling seemed to show not only in his mode of dress, but in his physiognomy. You might take the coachmen, the groom and the ostler a hundred miles from their stables, dress them, disguise them, and there was still something of the horse about them. They could leave the stables and horses, and twenty years later there remained some indefinable thing which marked them and revealed their one-time occupation.

Croxley Green Laundry cart in New Road

74

Proud figures were the coachman and cabby, with their silk toppers and their breeches. They took equal pride in themselves and the vehicles they managed. About this time a new figure began to be seen in the streets: the motor car driver. He too soon acquired a dress which marked him out as the custodian of the new-fangled machine, and his peaked cap, goggles, gauntlet gloves and brightly-polished leather gaiters were the very latest thing in uniforms.

Still to be seen in the street were many varied characters who still followed trades and occupations which had existed for many, many years. These tradesmen needed no workshop, for they knocked on doors, called their occupations, and dealt with the work given them on the path in front of the house. The travelling tinker, the grinder of knives, scissors, razors, and all tools that needed a sharp edge, these had been persistent figures on the roads of England for many years. The grinder's equipment, little changed through the centuries, was a familiar sight in both town and country, and an object of interest to most

 small boys. His call of 'Knives to grind, scissors to grind' usually secured him some jobs to do, but also the less welcome audience of youngsters who always found these itinerant workers an escape from boredom and a free show which never palled. The whirling treadle-propelled wheel and the screech of steel on sandstone was a great crowd-puller.

Flatterers too were these gentlemen, and often when the housewife gave them her scissors to be sharpened they would return them declaring they hadn't sharpened such another piece of steel for years, and compliment her on her acuteness in having purchased such an implement. They assured her it was a pleasure to put an edge on a real piece of Sheffield steel, and they only wished their other customers had been equally discerning when buying their cutlery.

The tinker would repair many articles of domestic use. He would solder leaks in kettles, baths and saucepans, and could put a new tin or copper bottom on any cooking pot with a speed and skill which amazed the bystander.

Another old tradesman still to be seen working in the village street was the chair-maker. Like the tinker he had been a well known sight and a useful servant of the community for many years. These 'chair-doctors' always carried chairs on to the pavement in front of the house to do the job, for in this way they were seen by neighbours and passers-by, and this sometimes led to their obtaining more work. They were wonderfully quick and deft at replaiting rush or straw seats, but these seats were often replaced by yellow varnished seats made from plywood, patterned out with ventilating holes. These plywood seats were carried and fixed by the chairmender in the days when his work was swiftly declining, and this probably contributed to his eventual disappearance. The resourceful housewife soon found that she could easily buy and fix them for herself, and would soon cease to employ the chairmender, who had to be paid a few precious coppers for the job.

The mat mender, too, after perhaps several centuries of service to the homes of England, was still going his rounds, but his trade, like that of the chair-mender, was an ever-decreasing one. He knocked at the door with his mat-mending fibres draped over his shoulders. A quick glance at the mat when the door was opened, and he was able to assess his chances of getting a job. If the doormat showed signs of wear in the middle, or was beginning to fray at the edges, he had spotted this as soon as the door opened and had given an estimate for the job before the mat could be lifted from the ground. This he always increased after a closer inspection. If he was given the job, he too would decline to carry it out at the back door, but carried it into the road and sat at the kerb to do the work, hoping that some of those who saw him at work would bring him more jobs to do.

But most fascinating of all the road-side workers was the mender of plates and glassware. He was surely the most skilled craftsman of this fading band of travelling tradesmen. Seated tailor-fashion at the kerb, he would patiently drill a fragile plate with the unusual drill used by these craftsmen. While one hand held the plate, the other sawed sideways, holding a wooden bow, whose string was wound round the stem of the drill. As the bow moved, so the drill rotated, and with this crude piece of equipment I have often seen delicate china repaired so that the original break was scarcely visible. Each half would be drilled at least twice, and then rivets inserted in the holes, which were always exactly opposite each other, as though placed with the aid of delicate equipment – as perhaps they were but the delicacy lay in the fingers and eyes of the worker. Even now, on many a dresser, sideboard or wall you may find traces of the china and glass mender. Look at that ornamental plate with the faint hair-line across its face. Take it down and hold it up to the window, and you will see two metal rivets showing as dark shadows in the translucent china. Treat it gently, for the workman will not be calling again.

If we welcomed the tinker and grinder for entertainment value, and the plate-mender to admire his skill, one other caller was more eagerly awaited and more joyfully received than either – the muffin man. The long summer days had passed and winter was not far off when we first heard the distant tinkle of the muffin bell and its promise of many a scrumptious tea. From now until the spring through all the cold winter days we would listen with mouth-watering anticipation for the call of that bell. When the dusk began to fall on those dull misty, winter afternoons, the fire seemed to burn brighter through the bars of the kitchen range as if it, too, delighted in its promised task of toasting the golden muffins. The very kettle simmering on the hob seemed to gargle a cheerier note. Now the louder notes of his bell gave warning that the muffin-man was

drawing near, and we hastened to the window to watch his approach with his tray of muffins skilfully balanced on his head. The tray now balanced on fence or window-sill, he began to remove the covering cloths: first the waterproof one, then the green baize, and finally the white one that covered the muffins.

The price settled and the money paid, the puffy muffins were carried in triumph to the hearth, where two large dinner plates were prepared for their reception. Now each muffin in turn was impaled on the long three-pronged telescopic toasting fork, removed when it had been toasted a golden brown on each side and liberally plastered with butter: a tea which was always eagerly awaited and never failed to satisfy.

Came the winter when we waited in vain for the tinkling of the well-loved bell. He never came again. Muffin man, tray and bell had all passed into oblivion. From then on when the alluring smell of toasting muffins mingled with the steam of the kettle, they would have been purchased from the bakers. Where did the muffin man go? He didn't even say 'Goodbye'. Where were his tray and bell last placed? The bell would surely refuse to ring for anything less than those heavenly muffins. Perhaps more mystifying still, where did the muffin man come from? Such muffins were never baked in an ordinary bakery. Indeed, one wonders if either man or muffins could have been of earthly origin, for how did they contrive to be outside <u>everyone's</u> front door just as dusk was falling on a cold winter's afternoon?

The paper mill paid its workers' wages on Wednesdays, and on Thursday a varied assortment of callers arrived in the village determined to part its residents from their hard-won earnings. If you were the tenant of one of the company's houses your rent was deducted from your wage-packet, but if your house belonged to a private landlord then he didn't leave it too late on Thursday before arriving for his dues.

All those with whom the villagers dealt streamed into the village on Thursday morning. By eight o'clock in the morning appeared hawkers of fruit and vegetables, the fishmonger, and a host of lesser traders who hawked most of the commodities needed by the housewife of the time. The greengrocers and fishmongers travelled in their carts, often with their wives sitting on the tailboard. They seemed to manage to arrive at the beginning of our long village street together, all having come from the nearby market town. Great was the confusion as they hustled and bustled and called their wares with the full strength of their early-morning voices. Later in the day they would become more subdued and husky. The greengrocer still hawking his fruit and vegetables and extolling their wares is the only one who survives in the village to the present day.

Most pitiful of all the doorstep salesmen was the seller of small wares. These were mainly men, with an occasional woman, and they carried their stock-in-trade in a small suitcase. The entire stock could have been worth only a few shillings. They surely must have depended more on gifts which their apparent poverty might extract from the householder than on profit from their merchandise. On opening their cases at the back door they exposed a few articles then in daily use: collar studs, tie pins, papers of pins and safety pins, cards of wool, and a few combs, or perhaps a few yards of elastic and tapes, some hair slides, and a few pairs of men's braces and women's garters. All had harrowing tales to tell of misfortune and distress, both to themselves and to their families. Some were no doubt impostors, but in many cases their tales were probably true. This was a time of much hardship and poverty.

Some of these packmen carried cards enumerating their dependent relatives, their complaints and disabilities. The cards, which had the appearance of having been in regular use for many years, were grubby and finger-marked. The possessors of these cards, I always felt, were more insincere than the others, the least deserving of this class of callers.

A regular feature of the streets was the singer or player of some musical instrument. Few days passed without some of these soliciting for coppers. Of all the people who came to our village, these entertainers were the most diverse and multifarious. Perhaps the majority of them were individualists, lone rangers like the tramps, but there were many in pairs or even in larger groups. Some sang loudly and brashly, while others were too timid or too feeble in the vocal chords to raise their voices above a croaking whisper. Some would boldly take up a position in the middle of the road, hoping thereby to be handy to receive the offerings of passers-by on either pavement. Others would shuffle along in the gutter, cap in hand, and grateful to the few who crossed the road to give them something.

Some of these men were genuine entertainers who gave a good performance, sang well, and brought a little colour into the drab lives of many of those that heard them. They sang many of the sentimental ballads of the day, so popular with the ladies, and it was surprising how many doors would open to toss a copper, which most of the donors could ill afford to give away.

The musicians played a variety of instruments, violin, cornet and flute being the most common with the solo performer. Like many of the tramps they seemed to have regular rounds, and appeared at regular intervals. Occasionally a band consisting of four or five members would play. They did not wait to be given money by the passing public, but knocked at doors and thrust their collecting-box at the householder. Then there was the Italian with his barrel-organ. There were usually three or four of these together. They always seemed to be in a hurry, but managed to spare the time to give a loud knock on all the doors. All these men claimed to be entertainers, and such money as they were given was regarded as being payment for services rendered. For many of the women donors, however, it was hush-money, for with the mill on shift work many of their husbands were in bed, and apt to be somewhat peevish if wakened by the strains of a barrel organ in the middle of the morning.

There was another class of these folk who were in reality beggars, their attempts to sing being simply a means to expose their poverty and excite the pity of those that saw them. Sometimes they would be man and wife together, the man trying to sing and the woman acting as collector. Sometimes, too, they would have a child or so with them. All miserably dressed in the oldest and filthiest of clothing, they would be treated with great liberality by many of the tender-hearted women, often being given food and clothing in addition to money. It is doubtful if they ever wore any good clothing they were given – it would find its way to the second-hand shop. It was their business to look poor, and any improvement in their appearance would have led to a reduction in their takings.

Another way of obtaining a precarious livelihood was the sale of Old Moore's Almanac[35], and there were many men hawking these. Few households could be without their Old Moore – and he was always being quoted, and was a second Bible to many. Old Moore in the eyes of many could not be wrong: his predictions never failed. An earthquake in Peru, droughts in India, the death of some famous person, or the winner of the Derby; there was always someone ready to claim that it had been foretold by the oracle. Probably they were right, as there were many editions of this almanac on sale from different publishers, all with varying predictions – and all claiming to be the original article.

The almanac sellers were a nondescript crowd of individuals. There was intense competition to be the first on the rounds with a new edition, and between the rival original publishers to beat each other into print. As a result each year's issue arrived about twelve months in advance. Each new issue was bought by the salesmen from the

---

[35] Annual publication in the UK containing prophecies of the events of the following year. It was first published in 1700 under the title Vox Stellarum/Voices of the Stars, by Francis Moore (1657-c. 1715), an astrologer in the court of King Charles II. The Hutchinson Unabridged Encyclopedia. www.credoreference.com/entry/heliconhe/old_moore_s_almanac accessed 14 Feb 2012

publisher by the hundred or the thousand, according to the money available, and the crop of hopeful salesmen once more arrived at our doors.

Two other callers I remember from those far-off days were both women: the lavender seller and the gypsy woman. I do not recall just when the lavender woman called, but it was probably in late summer and autumn after the crop had been picked. Ours, I felt, would not have been the best of areas for selling lavender, as many would have grown it in their own gardens, but in the hope of making it more desirable to the ladies it had been made up into little sachets, and the women must have made some sales, for they were regular callers for many years.

Of all the multifarious hordes of street traders and door-to-door callers the most persistent, the most difficult to turn away empty-handed, was the gypsy woman. Arriving at the door she wheedled, whined, coaxed and intimidated many a poor woman who tried to resist her blandishments into parting with some money. These gypsies played on the fears of some and on the weakness of others for having their fortunes told, and were the least desirable of all the callers. Carrying a basket containing clothes pegs which they had made themselves, they would attempt to ingratiate themselves with a housewife by calling her a 'pretty lady' or telling her that she had a 'nice kind face'.

The pegs, though crude by modern standards, were the product of a real old rural craft, and were made at great speed by these wanderers. Sometimes they could be seen at work on the fringe of some wayside copse, the entire family assisting in the operation. Peg selling was their excuse for calling, and while they were always pleased enough to sell a dozen or two, they made more money with their wheedling tongues, parting many a poor woman from shillings she could ill afford by filling her head with a lot of nonsense. The gypsy woman was the last of the old travellers to knock at the door, and latterly her basket no longer contained wooden pegs, but plastic ones, or some trashy article purchased from the chain store simply to capture the interest of the housewife and make an opening for story-telling. For generations the wife was the most prominent of the gypsy family, and the male members were seldom seen, but in recent years the men seem to have become scrap iron dealers, and are often seen in twos and threes.

81

In less than half a century this host of callers, once an everyday sight, have disappeared one by one. Their visits grew less frequent, and finally ceased altogether.

Travellers' joy in a Croxley hedgerow

CHAPTER ELEVEN

Village gossip

Mrs Tullet lived in the neighbouring town of Rickmansworth. Her husband was related to my father, but the exact relationship I was never able to find out. If asked, my mother (something of an amateur genealogist) would launch forth into a long and involved explanation in which most of the neighbouring towns and villages were mentioned, and hosts of uncles, aunts and cousins, their places of residence, the families they married into, and the families they should have married into.

Most of these relations had died long before my time, and I gave up trying to unravel such a long and complex tale. This was more especially so as my father's explanation, though much briefer, seemed to satisfy all enquirers. On the one or two occasions when I heard some interested party enquire of him just what <u>was</u> Mrs Tullet's connection with the family he said tersely, 'Her cat shit on our doorstep'. They never seemed to ask again.

I remember thinking it fortunate that it was <u>her</u> cat and <u>our</u> doorstep, and not our cat and her doorstep. Had it been the other way around it would surely have broken the slender threads that bound us, for Mrs Tullet was the cleanest, most fastidious person I had ever seen. Cleanliness was almost a religion with her, and all her waking hours seemed spent in washing, dusting and polishing.

It was her habit to walk up from her home on a Tuesday afternoon, and she generally arrived at our house about three o'clock, when she perched herself on the very edge of a chair and invariably remarked, 'I've just come out for a walk, and thought I would drop in for a moment'. This statement was always received with an internal groan by any of the family who happened to be present, for it meant that she would be staying at least three hours, during which time she would refuse the proffered cup of tea and keep her coat on, to maintain the pretence that she was about to depart.

She was the most inquisitive, quarrelsome gossip, and at the same time the most patriotic person I have ever met. How she was able to acquire all the gossip which ranged over three or four villages I shall never know, for she added little to her store during her visits to us. The moment she arrived she began to regale my mother with all her bits of confidential information (which were on no account to be repeated). Any attempt to confirm, contest, or make any comment at all was politely ignored while she gobbled ceaselessly on.

The Tullets owned several houses, which were the cause of many disputes between her and the tenants, the slightest repair involving voluminous correspondence. Always she knew the reason for any repair being necessary. Should a heavy fall of snow bring down a length of gutter, the tenant received a strongly-worded letter pointing out that it wasn't the snow that was responsible, but the tenant's son, who had been seen bouncing a ball against the gutter. If a chimney stack needed repointing, it wasn't because of natural decay, but because a passing pigeon had rested there and been pecking at the mortar.

Despite our slight relationship, Mrs Tullet and my mother always used each other's surnames (on the rare occasions when my mother was able to join the conversation at all, that is), and Mrs Tullet was constantly mentioning Mr Tullet. Sometimes, too, she talked about someone called Cyril. It was a curious thing, but when any disagreement with a tenant required a stiff letter or, more awful still, a personal call, this was always carried out by Cyril. She would describe all this in detail, 'And so I said to Cyril, "We're not having that. Only last September they had a new slate on the roof – we can't afford to keep renewing slates, you'll have to go round and put them in their place"'. Or perhaps a tap needed a new washer or a pipe sprang a leak: any of these minor repairs could bring them into conflict with Cyril, and always he routed his enemies and emerged triumphant.

Now Mr Tullet was the meekest, mildest and most insignificant little man, and I thought how lucky Mrs Tullet was to have Cyril as a champion to defeat all her detractors. Cyril was also most elusive. I tried to catch a glimpse of him when we passed her home, or on our rare visits there. So easily did he dispose of her foes; so completely vanquished were all those who dared to engage in combat that I felt sure he must be at least six feet tall and possessed of every human virtue. After listening to so many of his exploits I had built up a mental picture of him which I always conjured up when she spoke of Cyril, and he was by far the finest, fittest, most handsome man I 'knew' – in striking contrast to poor undersized, self-effacing Mr Tullet. How, I wondered, did he come to live with the Tullets? Was he Mrs Tullet's brother? He couldn't be Mr

Tullet's brother for he, poor man, could never have a brother of Cyril's class.

On a never-to-be-forgotten afternoon Mrs Tullet arrived breathing fire and vengeance. A tenant goaded beyond endurance by some rotting floorboards which he had been endeavouring to get renewed for some years, had had the effrontery to call on the Tullets. Worse still, after some verbal exchanges the enraged tenant had actually struck Mr Tullet. Where, I wondered, was Cyril? How easily he would have dealt with this situation.

Still Mrs Tullet ranted on, and while she raved and I listened in childish wonder, the astounding truth became clear to me: Cyril and Mr Tullet were one and the same person. Cyril the tall, the handsome paragon, the elusive Cyril, was a figment of my own creation. I had, childlike, been unable to see Mr Tullet defeating his opponents so easily and casually; had forgotten that grown-ups, too, had Christian names, and so created my own Cyril. Whatever the reason, the loss of my Cyril was a severe blow to me, and thereafter Mrs Tullet's brushes with the tenants lost their interest. Mr Tullet still emerged victorious, but one at least of her listeners disbelieved it. I could still see Cyril carrying all before him, but not downtrodden Mr Tullet.

Having arrived at about three o'clock, it was about four-thirty when Mrs Tullet first remarked, 'I shall have to be getting along', and began to prepare for her departure by taking up an even more precarious position on the edge of the chair. Half an hour later, still retaining her balance on the chair, she would interrupt her flow of gossip with, 'I really will have to be off and get Mr Tullet's tea.' Eventually she would stand up, but still continue the conversation.

When she got to her feet my mother, who was usually seated about a yard away, arose too. Now they were both standing, a foot or so apart, with Mrs Tullet still talking. Slowly, almost imperceptibly, she would back to the door into the scullery, and my mother, just as slowly but surely, would follow. Soon Mrs Tullet's hand, which had been reaching for the door-knob on the living-room side found it. This was a position she could hold for another twenty minutes or so. Next she would gradually open the door and transfer her hand from the living-room side to the scullery side. My mother, who had followed her closely all the time, now grasped the door-knob relinquished by her visitor and both ladies held the same door, one from one side and one from the other. This position was maintained for some minutes, until Mrs Tullet's hand left the outer handle, when my mother rapidly grasped it.

Mrs Tullet now began a slow retreat of some three or four feet to the door leading on to the garden. This required a few more minutes, until she found the back door-knob, when the performance at the other door was repeated. If it was raining, snowing, or generally unpleasant weather, Mrs Tullet would now put up her umbrella and abruptly depart. If, however, it was a nice day, my mother would have to pursue her to the front garden gate.

I used to wonder what would have happened had my mother begun to retreat instead of occupying each position vacated by the departing visitor. Would Mrs Tullet, I wondered, have then moved forward again, until she finally regained her chair?

✣✣✣ CHAPTER TWELVE ✣✣✣

The sporting miller – the Holloway family[36]

The Holloways were a noted sporting family in the village for many years. Ephraim Holloway bought Croxley windmill in 1877, and ran the mill until his death in 1890, but important as the miller was in those days, Ephraim was as well known for his cricket. He played for the village team for many years, but in sporting prowess he was outshone by his son Jim. Born in 1879, Jim Holloway was the doyen of Croxley Green cricket – the demon bowler of Croxley Green.

Jim was forty-three years a playing member of the side, and for twenty-six of those years he was captain. In the record books are plentiful records of his achievements, with 'bowled J. Holloway' constantly recurring. Jim once took nine wickets for one run, while in another year he captured a hundred wickets between May 1st and the end of August in Saturday cricket alone. He was seventy when he made his last bow as a player, and the analysis in the scorebook shows, fittingly, 'J. Holloway: 2 wickets for 0 runs'.

Jim's brothers Frank and Horace also played for the club, and by the time of Jim's retirement from the active list (and even then he remained Chairman of the club) his son was a team member. It was in a very different sport, however, that the family gained a further distinction: one they might not be quite so keen to remember, although the story is still told with relish in the pubs of the village.

Pigeon racing was becoming a large and well-organised sport just after the First World War, and there was much interest in it in Croxley Green. One of the Holloway brothers (no names, no pack drill) was responsible for introducing a significant change in the rules. He had entered a bird for a trophy race – one carrying also a substantial cash prize. The pigeon, along with several other local entries, was despatched by rail to the releasing point, and the Croxley owners counted the hours to the return of their fancied entrants.

---

[36] See *Rickmansworth Historian,* 11, pp. 267-271

Croxley Windmill 1855 by R. J. Walsh

Long before they were expected, the Holloway entry flapped its way tiredly round the Mill, was spotted, and, as its owner rushed excitedly out, alighted in the upper branches of a nearby tree. Now, to claim the prize it was necessary to produce the ring from the bird's leg, as well as a certificate of the time home. The pigeon-loft was opened, but the pigeon remained in the tree. Grain was sprinkled on the ground, and the anxious owner made clucking noises. There was no movement from the bird, which now seemed to have gone to sleep. No doubt it was tired by its journey.

The precious minutes were ticking away, and the owner became more and more distraught. The prize, he was sure, was almost within his grasp, yet the pigeon still rested comfortably out of reach. There was no time to fetch a ladder, and in any case this would probably have frightened the bird into changing its perch. He took a quick decision, rushed indoors for a moment, and within seconds after returning had the bird in his hands – shot.

The ring was removed from the corpse, and crime in this instance paid for the prize was won, but somehow the story got about. Perhaps some other Croxley owner might have won but for the flash of Holloway quickness of mind. In any event, the rules as they stood then said nothing against owners shooting their birds. The sporting press took the matter up, and the rules were altered. Since then the winner of any prize must be able to produce his bird, alive and well, before the trophy is awarded.

An old rhyme runs,
> *Blow wind, blow, and go Mill, go!*
> *That the Miller may grind his corn!*
> *That the Baker may bake it*
> *And into bread make it.*
> *And bring us a loaf in the morn.*

Frank Holloway, who owned the Mill in the early years of this[37] century, was also Croxley's baker, and brought us many 'a loaf in the morn', but the Mill will grind no more, and our bread comes to us today wrapped in greaseproof paper and baked many miles away. But perhaps on still summer afternoons on the old cricket ground, across the main road from the Red House, in between the rattle of the trains that now cross it on their way to London, you will hear, very faintly, a cry of 'Zat!' as some long-vanished batsman is 'Bowled J. Holloway, 0'.

---

[37] i.e. twentieth century

CHAPTER THIRTEEN

Passing the time of day

'He's gone, then.'

'Ah, and I reckon he's gone for good this time – 'e's took 'is darts with 'im.'

'Of course, he's been poorly for a long time.'

'Oh ah! Last time she brought 'im 'ome from 'ospital they'd took so many things out she reckoned she needed a trap to fetch 'im and Colin Taylor's big cart for the spare parts.'

'I saw him at his brother's funeral six month's back and he didn't look well then.'

'I know. I spoke to 'im arterwards, and I said to 'im, "You're not lookin' too bright yourself Dick"', I said, 'an' 'e said, "I ent feelin' too bright, neither. I reckon it'll be my turn next", 'e said, so I says to 'im, "Ain't 'ardly worth your while goin' back 'ome, is it?", and 'e laughed.'

'I think she's been expecting him to go.'

'Oh, yes. Only last week she went to 'im in the evening, just to see if 'e was still there, and she said to 'im then, "If you do pop off in the night, be sure and blow the candle out."'

'The funeral was delayed, though wasn't it?'

'Ah. Coffin wadn't ready.'

'Whyever not?'

'Old Woody wadn't worried. 'E never is. "I don't reckon Dick'll mind waiting," 'e said to me. O'course, 'e's always late with 'is jobs. I reckon if it was left to 'im all our coffins'd be too late for Resurrection Day.'

'It seems strange, after all the illness he's had, to go off suddenly with 'flu – just like Stalin!'

'Oo?'

'Stalin, you know, <u>Joseph</u> Stalin.'

'No, I've lived in Croxley forty years, and straight, I don't know a dozen people.'

'But it was a very nice funeral.'

'Oh ah. Couldn't 'ave 'ad a better. But I'll tell you one thing.'

'What's that?'

'It's the first time ole Dick's been on the bier with 'er consent.'

Bricket Wood Fair

'I ain't got no time for women,' he said, 'Ain't never 'ad. I kept myself to myself, and I don't reckon I missed much.'

'What, even when you were a lad?'

'All me life, I reckon – excepting the Sunday School treat at Bricket Wood.'

'But you'd be better off now with a wife to look after you.'

'What do I want with a wife? I got a pension book.'

'Well, that may be alright in the Post Office, but that ain't much use to go to bed with.'

'Anyway, I'm a gardener. It don't take me long to do an hour in the garden, but I don't reckon I got time for a wife as well.'

'Adam was a gardener, and he had a wife.'

'Ah, but he didn't keep his job long arter he had her!'

CHAPTER FOURTEEN

Croxley Mummers[38]

Thomas Hughes wrote in *Tom Brown's Schooldays*, 'The first dramatic performance Tom ever saw was the mummer's play, performed by the local boys at his home in the Berkshire Downs. He remembered it with affection all his life'.

I like to think that somewhere there may be men and women who look back to their childhood and the visits we Croxley Mummers made to their homes, and remember them, too, with affection those Christmas Eves.

Croxley Mummers at Parrotts

---

[38] See Frank Paddick's more detailed account in the *Rickmansworth Historian,* 8, pp.175-184 which includes the text of the Mummers' play and this quotation:
'To shorten winter sadness, see where the folk with gladness
    Disguised all are coming right wantonly a-mumming.'
The drawings are taken from R J Walsh's illustrations to that article.

It was shortly after the First World War that 'Neggy' Wilson realised a long-cherished dream: the revival of a Mummers Troupe in the village. The first gathering of aspiring mummers had one thing in common: they had all shown some histrionic skill in the school's annual Christmas concert. They were well chosen, too, for several, Stan Lyons, Fred Randall, the brothers Jim, George and Bill Samuels and I, were to remain the hard core of the Croxley Mummers for the next forty years. Many came and went, but this little band stayed on.

Our early mumming days were chaotic: we toured the village and performed by chance wherever a patron was willing to receive us. It was not long before we decided to perform by appointment only, and to this end delivered the following letter, written I am sure by 'Neggy':

Sir,

We beg leave to ask you, whom we know as one who believes in Christmas, and observes both in spirit and letter all its attendant traditional customs, who would not have it shorn of even one of the very least of them, to receive us – 'Ye Olde Mummers' as heretofore, on the Eve of its Feast under your hospitable rood [roof?], and permit us to unfold to you the old yet ever new 'Mummers Tale' which has given entertainment and instruction to our forebears of countless generations and will ever continue to do so. It is the same, the very same, there is but one – the only one – to play any other would be gross sacrilege, a grievous affront to Christmas, and of this no loyal self-conscious mummers would be guilty, it would make both them and their hosts the sport of avenging goblins.

We soon began to acquire traditions. It became traditional to make the Vicarage our first call and 'Lindiswara'[39], the home of the mill manager Charles Barton-Smith, the last one. This pattern remained for

---

[39] The site is now occupied by the flats 'Lindiswara Court' on Watford Road.

several years. The French family was at 'The Firs'[40] when we first went a-mumming, and Sir Frederick Heaton[41] became our patron there when they left. I remember much in forty years, but the most abiding memories of the early days were the bright lights of 'Waterdell House' and the final comfort of the library at 'Lindiswara'.

Preparation would begin some weeks before Christmas. Masks would need repairing and new costumes sometimes had to be made, while new mummers would have to be rehearsed. Each Christmas we felt that at last we had attained perfection, and each year some unexpected event required a hasty reshuffling of parts. Twice I recall the noble St. George failing to arrive and a new one stepping into the breach with his script concealed behind the knight's shield. Other parts were hastily rehearsed or perfected as we stumbled across the unlit Green.

We would assemble in the Boys' School, and emerge partially in costume with our masks and other paraphernalia considered indispensable to mumming. On arrival round about six o'clock at the Vicarage we gave our first performance to the evening's smallest audience, the Rev. Bloiss-Bishop, his wife and one or two maids. We were soon ready to depart and the vicar would accompany us to the door with 'Good night gentlemen, and a Merry Christmas – and, by the way, the Colonel has been on the telephone to know if you have started on your rounds and hopes you will not be late again this year'.

Round by the church and across the Green to 'Elmcote'[42], then Mr. Adams' home, we went, and here the words of the Wassailing song which we sometimes sang as we approached the houses really had some significance:

---

[40] The Firs is located on the opposite side of Sarratt Lane from the high wall around the grounds of Croxley House.

[41] Sir Frederick Heaton, chairman of the bus company Tillings who was living at 'The Firs' when he died. See John Hibbs, 'Heaton, Sir (John) Frederick (1880– 1949)', *Oxford Dictionary of National Biography*, Oxford University Press, 2004 [http://www.oxforddnb.com/view/article/41020, accessed 9 March 2011]

[42] Opposite the end of New Road.

Wassail! Wassail! Over the town,
Our toast it is white, our ale it is brown:
Our bowl it is made of the white maple tree.
With our wassailing bowl we drink to thee.

Come, butler, bring us a bowl of the best,
And we hope your soul in Heaven may rest.
But if you do draw us a bowl of the small
Then down will go butler, bowl and all.

The performance over, Mr. Graver, the butler, handed glasses all round but whether of the small or the best I was not in those youthful days qualified to judge. We were conscious by now that we were falling a little behind schedule, and the butler's parting message didn't help much. 'Mr. Adams just told me to tell you that the Colonel has been enquiring if you arrived on time, and hopes you will not be later than you promised.'

With a 'Merry Christmas' to the 'Elmcote' household; master, mistress, maids, guests, butler and all, we were once more out on the Green, making for Copthorne Road and the home of the Casebourne family. A real large party awaited us here: this was Dingley Dell itself, complete with grandmas who insisted on kissing all the Mummers in the best Pickwickian way. We were now painfully aware that our carefully planned timetable had broken down, and it was with some trepidation that we approached Parrotts and the awaiting Colonel. However, the Christmas spirit prevailed, and after a short lecture on the virtues of punctuality, St. George was soon defeating his adversaries in a house that must surely have witnessed the Mummers' Play in many bygone years.

On to the Green once more, and on our way to Little Green and Waterdell House. Perhaps it was the extra darkness of Little Green Lane beside the towering walls of Croxley House, but the lights of Waterdell always seemed especially bright. But perhaps it was the warm welcome of kindly Mrs. Forbes, who would meet us in the hall with a large box of chocolates and an oft-repeated request to 'Have a choc-choc, boys!'. Then round the great wall of Croxley House we would go to 'The Firs', where the family and staff gave us another warm welcome and the dogs barked in frantic resentment at the motley throng invading the house on Christmas Eve.

'The Firs' was usually our last engagement on the Green, and now began the long trek to Watford Road and 'Lindiswara'. If it was quiet when we went up the Green it was doubly so when we returned. Now even the feeble gaslight in the Coach and Horses and Artichoke had been put out and the last of their customers had departed. Each Christmas brought some fresh adventure – some long-remembered incident. Who of us will forget the night when hearing distant footfalls, we recognized the approach of that great old character Nabby Sear? Quickly concealing ourselves behind the hedge we waited, and then the dragon pounced out when Nabby drew level. Cast in the mould of St. George, it took more than a dragon to frighten that sturdy old farmer and we were promptly told to 'Be off wi' ye and take that bloody old moke wi' yer'.

It was drawing near to midnight when we kept our last appointment at 'Lindiswara'. The performance over, we needed no second invitation by our host to make ourselves at home and enjoy the Christmas fare provided, and finally relax in a haze of smoke from the large box of 'Passing Cloud'[43] which, in the words of the Doctor, 'had been left all ready near to hand'.

We had been on the road some six or seven hours and St. George had fought many battles with his tireless foes. How attractive was the comfort of 'Lindiswara' to us tired and aching Mummers, and how reluctantly we wished the family a Merry Christmas and went out into the cold Christmas morning. It was a bedraggled band of Mummers who made their way to their several homes through the deserted village.

---

[43] A brand of cigarettes produced by W.D.& H.O.Wills.

96

CHAPTER FIFTEEN

Our Village

"If I have sayed amiss I am content that any man amends it, or if I have sayed too little, any man that will to add what hym pleaseth to it." Roger Aschan[44]

A local historian seeking material turns to church and churchyard, to town hall or civic centre. Croxley Green has no civic centre, and its church is of no great age. The place itself has been called a 'village without a history', but the words are meaningless. Here in the Gade valley are the traces of Stone Age man. Our woods and lanes once echoed to the clatter of Cromwell's horse. My own generation saw and heard the Kaiser's Zeppelins, and felt the weight of Hitler's bombs. Great surgeons, soldiers, showmen and industrialists have made their homes amongst us, and our houses large and small are living history books.

---

[44] Ascham, Roger (1514/15–1568), author and royal tutor. See Rosemary O'Day, 'Ascham, Roger (1514/15–1568)', *Oxford Dictionary of National Biography*, Oxford University Press, 2004 [http://www.oxforddnb.com/view/article/732, accessed 9 March 2011]

Providence Hall

By repute the four oldest houses in the village were the four Halls: Red Hall in the Chandler's Cross Road; Providence Hall, delight of artist and photographer, at the entrance to the Dickinson sports ground; Croxley Hall, and Smoky Hall.

The last named has gone now. For centuries it stood, a red-brick farm-house at the south end of the Green.[45] Around it spread the cottages, farm buildings, windmill, bakehouse, storehouse, public houses, sawmill and smithy of the old village. Archie King, born in 1877 and for many years chief engineer at Croxley Mills, attended a dame school there in Smoky Hall's last years. It was run by 'Granny' Blackwell, whose husband had kept the Sportsman close by. Pupils ranged along both sides of a wooden table, Granny sat at the head reading the alphabet, aided by a long hazel stick with which, said Mr. King, she kept wonderful discipline.

After school, the children would linger to watch the sawyers at work in Windmill Lane, the smith at the forge by the Sportsman, or the silent grace of the windmill, then in its last days of sail.

Croxley Hall Farm

---

[45] Near the Sportsman Public House. See Frank Paddick's article 'In search of Smoky Hall' *Rickmansworth Historian*, 7, 1964 pp. 134-140.

The other Halls still remain. Stand on the railway bridge and look down into Croxley Hall Farm. It needs little imagination to people the yard with folk of bygone days. In 1530 the farm and its surroundings belonged to Cardinal Wolsey, in his position of Abbot of St. Albans. The barn stood there then, and is worth a look before it collapses.[46] It is disused now, and time is catching up with it, for our climate deals roughly with abandoned buildings, but Croxley Hall itself looks good for many years yet.

Our windmill, long associated with the Holloway family, has passed in living memory from wind to steam power, and now has been disused these many years. Even so, it served as a warden's post in Hitler's war, and still had a siren mounted on it until recently. The tower is still there, a house today, but still a prominent landmark.

In the houses round the Green have lived Professor Schafer,[47] pioneer of artifical respiration, the Du Maurier family,[48] Frank Curzon,[49] financier and impresario, and his actress wife Isobel Jay (who were later occupants of the house Schafer built[50]). The village gossips saw many newsworthy comings and goings – Ellaline Terriss, Seymour Hicks and Sir George Alexander[51] were among the regular visitors. In 1927

---

[46] The barn is in better condition today (2012).

[47] Schafer, Sir Edward Albert Sharpey, physiologist: see F. H. A. Marshall, 'Schafer, Sir Edward Albert Sharpey- (1850–1935)', rev. Anita McConnell, *Oxford Dictionary of National Biography*, Oxford University Press, 2004; online edn, Oct 2009 [http://www.oxforddnb.com/view/article/35967, accessed 9 March 2011]

[48] Du Maurier, Sir Gerald Hubert Edward Busson, actor, theatre manager and father of the author Daphne Du Maurier: see James Harding, 'Du Maurier, Sir Gerald Hubert Edward Busson (1873–1934)', *Oxford Dictionary of National Biography*, Oxford University Press, 2004; online edn, Jan 2011 [http://www.oxforddnb.com/view/article/32928, accessed 9 March 2011]

[49] Frank Curzon: mentioned in Du Maurier's biography. 'From 1910 to 1925, in partnership with Frank Curzon, Du Maurier managed Wyndhams Theatre, after which he joined Gilbert Miller at the St James's Theatre to direct and star in Frederick Lonsdale's *The Last of Mrs Cheyney* (1925), among others.'

[50] Little Gillions

[51] Ellaline Terriss was among the most successful musical comedy actresses of the late Victorian and Edwardian periods. See C. M. P. Taylor, 'Terriss, Ellaline [*real name* (Mary) Ellaline Lewin; *married name* (Mary) Ellaline Hicks, Lady

Curzon's horse 'Call Boy' won the derby, thus achieving a life time's ambition for his owner, who died within a few days of leading him into the visitor's enclosure.

17th September 1914, opened a new and more sober chapter in the history of Croxley Green. As dawn broke the villagers – mothers, brothers, sisters and sweethearts – began to gather round the Dickinson Institute. With Allied losses mounting on the Western front the Croxley Church Lads' Brigade had volunteered, almost to a man, and some thirty young men were leaving to join the King's Royal Rifle Corps. The bugle sounded, and as the mists rose over the Moor the little band marched from Croxley, soon to cross the Channel; all to acquit themselves with valour, many to be decorated, some never to return.

The Second World War found us all in the front line, with the destruction of many houses and of the Mission Hall, and severe damage to the church and many houses. Today the scars are largely healed, nature having helped repair the ravages of man.

The village has changed, inevitably, in the more than fifty years that I have lived here. In my boyhood we were an industrial island in a sea of great estates, surrounded as we were by the domain of my Lords of Essex, Clarendon and Ebury. This gave to the village a character unshared by our neighbours in West Herts – and the need to please the nobility gave Croxley Mills an 'Egyptian' façade to face Moor Park.

Hicks] (1871–1971)', *Oxford Dictionary of National Biography*, Oxford University Press, 2004; online edn, Jan 2011 [http://www.oxforddnb.com/view/article/40483, accessed 9 March 2011] She married Sir Seymour Hicks, actor, theatre manager, and author: see Richard Foulkes, 'Hicks, Sir (Edward) Seymour George (1871–1949)', *Oxford Dictionary of National Biography*, Oxford University Press, 2004; online edn, Jan 2011 [http://www.oxforddnb.com/view/article/33854, accessed 9 March 2011]

Sir George Alexander, [*real name* George Alexander Gibb Samson] actor and theatre manager: see J. P. Wearing, 'Alexander, Sir George (1858–1918)', *Oxford Dictionary of National Biography*, Oxford University Press, 2004; online edn, Jan 2011 [http://www.oxforddnb.com/view/article/30370, accessed 9 March 2011]

Bomb damage. Scots Hill

Croxley Mills "Egyptian" façade 1872-3

Our weather in those days came always from Will's Mother's[52] – our legendary weather-woman. 'It looks like rain over Will's Mother's'; 'It's bright over Will's Mothers'; 'It's cloudy over Will's Mother's'; were daily, if not hourly, remarks.

At the same time, it seemed to me, every event was measured from the Boer War, and Mafeking and Ladysmith were frequently cited. It was, 'Oh yes, that was when Ladysmith was relieved', or 'That would have been about the time of Mafeking', but we had, too, our own local undated event: 'the year the mill field grew turnips'. This was used as Sarah Camp used Mrs Harris, being brought in on every possible occasion to confuse and trap the unwary.

Our village street was very different then, and perhaps seems even more so because then behind the houses lay gardens, the orchards, and the back-fields, or to us boys 'the Backies' – my boyhood island in the sun. There I have gleaned in the corn-fields, made hay in the hay-fields, chased with dog and catapult the wild life in Fir Dell, Round Dell and The Spinney. Every hedge and every tree still remains clear in my memory: the holly bushes where the nightingales both sang and nested, the great beech tree with the little 'shooting hut' built in its shade, and the hedges and copses which furnished homes for so many of the wild birds we hunted, and prongs for the 'catties' with which we hunted them. The Backies were not only our haunt by day. We knew them too by moonlight, for most of our batfolding in the long winter nights was around these woods and fields.

Most of the Backies were in reality the fields of Parrotts, on the Green but some were farmed by a farmer living in New Road. To enable him to work them, a track was cut during my boyhood between Overton's Cottage and the next house. This divided Mr Overton's orchard in two, and left his house standing on a corner. Mr Overton must have been quite an old man when I knew him, and on fine sunny days his housekeeper would wheel him into the shrubbery in the front garden. He was very fat, and I cannot remember ever seeing him walk, but he

---

[52] Similar phrases are recorded in various parts of Britain on 'phrases.org.uk' – accessed on 31/10/2010. See also 'Oops, pardon, Mrs Arden!' *An embarrassment of domestic catchphrases,* by Nigel Rees (Robson Books, London 2001).

always carried a walking-stick in the wheel chair. This was no doubt intended for getting in and out of the chair, but he generally seemed to use it for rapping the hands of small boys who dared to scrape or touch his fence in passing. I remember buying apples and pears at the house, and no doubt the orchard had a cherry-tree as well, for many of the older houses thereabouts have white-heart trees even today, but our house, too, had its own cherry tree, so these we never bought.

The cart-track past Mr Overton's house is a road now, with Barton Way on the name-boards, and where he sat is the forecourt of our new County Library building, but it isn't so very long since another generation of village boys went scrumping in his orchard. It had changed hands by then, of course, and they called it 'Juicy Jackson's' but I don't doubt the apples tasted as good as in my day.

Mr. Overton was one of the many 'characters' who seemed then so plentiful in the village. Schoolmaster, doctor, mill manager, parson, were not only dignitaries, they were well enough known to us all to be personalities, and perhaps in our hasty age there isn't time for this kind of thing to happen. There are many more people living in Croxley Green now than ever before, and many of them work elsewhere, so they know less of each other than we did, but even allowing for the changed days, it seems that the individuals when I was a boy really <u>were</u> individuals.

Why, even the cats had characters. We shall never forget old Granny Gardner's ginger tom. Granny kept the little shop at our end of the village. In the window were displayed Everlasting Strips, Spanish Comfits, Sherbet Dabs, Vinegar Flats, 'Cally-bunkers', Bassidy Hard Juice, Cut Cavendish and Locust Beans. A poor-selling line were Locust Beans, as they could be obtained from the sheep-pens. But the 'piece de resistance' was a tall jar containing 'Lavender-scented Cashews – 4d. an ounce'. Fourpence an ounce in a window where most items were priced at a halfpenny or a farthing. Fourpence an ounce in an age were most things were bought by the bushel, popple or peck. They were far above our means, but it was rumoured they were bought in large quantities by the local gentry, while an ounce of lavender-scented cashews purchased by a hobbledehoy about to take the girl of his choice out for the first time was considered a master-stroke, and calculated to establish him as a man of impeccable taste. The cashews had the additional advantage of being so small that an ounce of them would last the entire evening.

103

Granny's window was on the sunny side of our village street, and it was here that her cat spent most of its days, shifting its position as the sun moved round. Hygiene, of course, was ignored and a cat's hair here or there was nobody's business. It was a cat of tiger-like proportions, placid enough unless provoked. We would tease it through the window-pane until it snarled and spat at us.

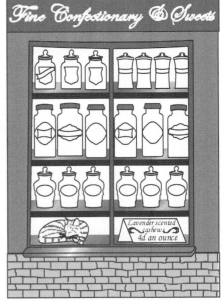

A new generation inhabits our village street. They have sawn down our trees, uprooted our shrubs and stripped the vines from the walls, and the noise of the lawn-mower and motor car disturbs the evening calm. We have been submerged by suburbia. The great oaks that lined the old road have been supplanted by concrete lamp-standards. The path that the reeling drunkard made from The Red House to the shelter of the great oak opposite now has a winking light at either side, and is called a zebra crossing. Where once pheasants called in the old pheasantry the porter now yells, 'All stations to Harrow, Wembley Park and Baker Street'. All our fields have been built over, and little of our rural character remains.

But disregarding all this, and the barometric pressure on the Air Ministry roof, our weather still comes from Will's Mother's and seems to point to a good Autumn. Another one, you know, like the year the Mill field grew turnips.

LIST OF ILLUSTRATIONS

---

[53] Thanks are due to those who have provided the illustrations. Every effort has been made to trace their provenance.
[54] *Rickmansworth a Pictorial History,* Adrienne and Christopher Jacques, Rickmansworth Historical Society 1996.

INDEX

107

Copthorne Cottages on the Green